What people say about James Dillehay's books

"The blueprint for success in the crafts industry."
The Crafts Report

"A useful compilation of 'insider information.'"
Woodshop News

"James is by far the most qualified and talented marketer for the craft industry. His knowledge is only outweighed by his honest desire to help people."
Phoebe Welburn, Welburn Gourd Farm

"Everything you need to know is here, and it's applicable to any craft."
Millennium Whole Earth Catalog

"Quite an expert....Very informative. I wish we could keep you for the next three days."
Carol Duvall, HGTV, The Carol Duvall Show

"James was a guest speaker on our Guerilla Marketing conference call and he blew me away with what he knows about selling."
Jay Levinson, best-selling author Guerrilla Marketing

"James was one of our most popular instructors at Sage-Ways, LLC, because he provided excellent information in an entertaining way. Customers often signed up for multiple classes with James because he gave them practical information they could put to use immediately."
Carole Douras, CEO: SageWays

"Dillehay knows the field — I can't think of a more rewarding retirement pursuit."
Jack Smith, Syndicated Columnist: Senior Sense

Make Money with
Wood Crafts

How to Sell on Etsy, Amazon, at Craft Shows, to Interior Designers and Everywhere Else, and How to Get Top Dollars for Your Wood Projects

JAMES DILLEHAY

Make Money with Wood Crafts

ISBN: 978-1-7320264-3-8
Warm Snow Publishers
PO Box 170
Torreon, NM 87061
Craftmarketer.com

Table of Contents

Stay up to date with what's working and what isn't in the handmade marketplace. Subscribe to James' newsletter at: **Craftmarketer.com/newsletter/**. You'll get news and action steps you can use to grow your crafts business.

Introduction

The book is about the business side of how to turn your love for woodworking into multiple income streams. It can help you whether you are just starting with a few ideas for making and selling wood crafts or if you have already sold some of your pieces and you want to grow.

Growing usually means expanding your product line and/ or your market reach. With this guide, you will discover where to get ideas for making wood crafts in demand and scaling your business to the size you want.

You will learn how to prepare your woodworking crafts for prime time; otherwise the later chapters on finding more shoppers to get your message in front of will be a waste of time and money. No amount of marketing will make a weak presentation convert browsers into buyers.

You will discover pricing formulas used by successful wood artisans that earn you optimal profit margins.

You will get tips for transforming your social connections into customers and ambassadors for your handcrafted products.

The advice, tactics, and resources here come from my over thirty years of making and selling my handmade products at events and shows, to stores and galleries from Manhattan to Sedona, on Etsy, Amazon, and eBay, and through my gift shop gallery near Santa Fe, New Mexico.

Many years ago, a woodworker friend offered me a job because his business was expanding. Through his friendship with an art broker, he got wealthy clients looking for top quality wood furnishings in their million dollar homes. We built and installed one mahogany door and frame that my friend billed out at $7,000.

Years later, when I had my gallery, art and crafts made from wood were among the top sellers because their makers used the marketing tactics you'll find in these pages. We sold lightweight wooden Christmas ornaments for around $15, wood framed jewelry from recycled materials for $150, and cedar-wood coffee tables for $750.

There is a world of opportunities for selling your hand-made products. The guidelines in this book will help you learn how to brand your craft business, price your products, set up for accepting payments, sell online at Etsy and elsewhere, scale up via wholesale, and much more.

Let's start at the beginning: gathering ideas for things to make. Get profitable from the start by discovering what buyers want and then making your own versions of what's hot in the marketplace.

CHAPTER 1

Wood Crafts to Make and Sell

There are thousands of possibilities for wood crafts to make to sell. This chapter shows you how to find ideas and how to prioritize them by products shoppers want.

Successful woodcrafters create a product line based on a theme or niche. For example, you might make lightweight painted Christmas ornaments from sections of wood or a line of ornately carved crosses. Or, you might specialize in larger pieces like coffee tables crafted from thick sections of cedar.

Develop one product line, determine its prime market (like Amazon Handmade, Etsy, craft shows, or galleries), and get sales coming in, before adding more products or markets.

Online e-commerce shops like Etsy may deliver better results for a lower-priced craft, while often, your high-end pieces will go into galleries or stores. In my gallery, we sold high-end and low-end wood crafts. We moved a lot of small pieces like wood ornaments at $15 and larger items like tables for $500.

We'll talk more about each kind of market throughout the book. For now, let's start with:

- How to find wood craft product ideas
- How to test-market your product idea to shoppers.
- Ways to make your product line stand out from others.

* * * * *

The following section reveals how to research markets for product ideas already selling. Do not copy others' work. It's unethical and you can lose your online web presence or, worse, be sued for copyright infringement. Use the sources here to brainstorm ideas from which you will craft your own unique pieces.

* * * * *

How to Find Wood Craft Product Ideas

The first place to look for what's selling online is on Etsy and Amazon Handmade. We can use tools that gather search terms from buyers and produce reports that reveal shopping trends. EtsyRank.com is a subscription service providing reports on keywords used by real buyers on Etsy, Amazon, eBay, Pinterest, and Google Shopping.

Among the reports you can generate in EtsyRank is one called Trend Buzz. It provides data on the top searched for items on Etsy by category and overall in a recent 30-day period. Below is a list of the most popular Etsy searches for items in the "Home & Living" category that could be made from wood:

personalized gift: 195,702
farmhouse decor: 61,121
home decor: 53,079
wall decor: 48,572
room decor: 41,347
dining table: 31,092
cutting board: 29,798
wind chimes: 28,830
planter: 28,735
rolling tray: 24,624
furniture: 24,296
coasters: 23,998
office decor: 23,093
tray: 19,747
bird feeder: 18,290
spice rack: 17,634
plant stand: 17,216
wooden letters: 14,646
woodland nursery decor: 14,538

That's a lot of products consumers are looking for. And that's just on Etsy. Though EtsyRank also shows search data from Amazon, another tool, MerchantWords.com (subscription service) delivers a variety of reports for learning how Amazon buyers search and buy. Below are searches performed on Amazon (in a 30-day period) using the phrase "cutting board" in the "Handmade" category:

cutting board with pockets: 1,503
engraved cutting board set: 789
maple cutting board books: 600
yeti cutting board: 262
roller cutting board: 248
birds eye maple cutting board: 109
airstream cutting board: 105
wooden cutting board with handle for decoration: 92
mini wood cutting board with handle: 85
cutting board 12x10: 80
kitchen sink cutting board cover: 72

MerchantWords also revealed the number of searches in all categories (not just "Handmade") for "cutting board" was 818,764 in a month as I write this. That shows a strong over-all demand for cutting boards on Amazon. But you would want to stay in the "Handmade" category, because in the general Amazon marketplace, competing sellers list thousands of cheap, mass-produced items from China.

For both EtsyRank and MerchantWords, the number of searches shown is for a thirty-day period near the time of this writing. Do your own search for the most current data.

We'll go more into how to use the data you can gather from keyword search tools in the chapter on SEO.

More Ways to Find Product Ideas

You can also find product ideas by looking at Etsy and Amazon Handmade's categories. The categories and subcategories on both sites can provide clues to what is selling in the marketplace.

For examples, see: https://www.etsy.com/help/categories/seller. Under the category of Home & Living, there's a subcategory called Bath Tub Trays. Typing "bath tub trays" into the Etsy search bar brought up around 300 product listings, some of them showing hundreds of sales and positive reviews.

On Amazon, go to: https://www.amazon.com/Best-Sellers-Handmade/zgbs/handmade/ to view bestsellers in the Handmade category. The products you see there change hourly according to sales. But as I was writing this, the #2 bestselling item under Handmade and Home & Kitchen was a personalized wood cutting board.

Not only will you get product ideas from reviewing the subcategories themselves, you'll get a look at seller listings that are converting shoppers to buyers.

Pinterest.com is an excellent tool for learning what consumers want. Check out their Trends app at https://trends.pinterest.com/ At the time I write this "contemporary dining room" was a top search term and the example pin showing up was a picture of a handcrafted dining room table. Also see the related app, Pinterest Top 100 at https://www.pinterest100.com/.

You probably are aware of magazines like *Woodshop News, American Woodworker, Popular Woodworking*, and others. These publications not only help improve your skills, they can also be a source of product ideas. As mentioned above, the projects you come across can't be copied exactly, but when you find something you like, it's easy enough to make your own version.

From the steps above, start your own list of subcategories of products you could or want to make. Prioritize your ideas. Pick things you will enjoy making. You can be profitable with just one or two types of products. Later on, add new items as your business grows.

Don't forget your own creativity. Take a product idea that's popular and create your own artistic version. Make it different enough to brand as your own.

How to Test-Market Your Product Idea

No matter how great you (and your mom) think your ideas are, you can't survive or thrive in the business world without first testing and measuring how the buying public reacts to your work.

The fastest real-life testing ground for handmade products is to display them at two or three well-attended local craft shows. Craft shows allow you to get immediate feedback through shopper comments and sales, or not.

Another way to fast-check your idea is by posting on social sites like Instagram, Pinterest, and Facebook. Post images or videos of your products. Take notes about how your followers react.

Your social media contacts know you, or kind of know you, so they may give you positive encouragement. Many Etsy stores have grown their customer base starting with sales from friends, family, and social media connections.

Another powerful feedback trial is taking something you've made and walking into shops and galleries you think would be a suitable fit for your work. Start a conversation with a sales clerk or, better yet, the owner. Ask what they think. The feedback will be invaluable, even if it hurts your feelings.

Ways to Make Your Product Line Stand Out

After you have your product list, the next step is making things. You will probably have competition, so let's look at ways to craft products so they stand out from other sellers:

Personalization. Personalized gifts are very popular, both at shows and on Etsy. If appropriate for what you make, offer the option to add a recipient's name to an item for a premium price. Some top-sellers on Etsy and Amazon Handmade offer customizing or personalizing as an option. In May 2020, the search term "personalized gift" was searched for on Etsy 195,702 times. That's a consumer demand worth tapping into.

Your story. Your story is the connecting message. Shoppers want to do business with real people. Telling them your story separates you from mass-manufactured products.

Quality sells. Whatever you make, do it well. Quality work is obvious and attractive. My craft teacher used to say, "Your handwork doesn't lie. All your mistakes come back to haunt you."

Niches and Themes. Breaking into retail with a new line, you face a crowded market. To stand out, look for a low-competition niche area within a category. Think about themes. Many of your customers will have someone on their gift list who collects cars, dinosaurs, unicorns, elephants, gnomes, or other collectibles.

Inform shoppers if you use **sustainable materials**. Don't assume customers will know that you are a "green business." Point it out in promotional material like hangtags, packaging, websites, and booth displays.

Packaging. Packaging is another place to brand your business. It's also a way to use sustainable materials (call attention to this on your boxes and wrappers) as many companies that make packaging boxes and bags do so with recycled paper.

Eye-catching images. When listing your products online, your images do the selling (or not.) If there is any place in your business that justifies investing money, it is in getting great photos of your work.

Now that you know the basics for finding ideas to turn into popular items shoppers are looking for, you are one step closer to starting your venture. Next, you will need to get set up to accept payments, choose a catchy business name, and a few other things. Read on for how to get your new business started the right way.

CHAPTER 2

Setting Up to Make Sales

Before you can make sales, you need several things in place. This chapter explains the basic legal requirements for setting up your business to avoid future problems with the IRS and to make your gig operate more smoothly.

Here you will learn about:

- Choosing a name for your business
- Legal requirements: permits and licenses
- Accepting credit card payments
- Keeping records

Choosing a Name for Your Business

Your business needs a name that is short, catchy, and doesn't already belong to someone else.

Many makers use their own name as their business name. For one, it's more personal; shoppers can see you are an actual person standing behind your name.

Another plus for using your name is that it makes it easy for customers who have bought from you at events to recognize your name when it appears on their receipt and credit card statement. Occasionally, a shopper won't remember all the vendors she bought from and then may later dispute the charge after going over her credit card statement.

If you don't want to use your name, make a list of your favorite alternatives with the best one at the top. Wait a few days for your ideas to settle before reviewing your list. If you still like your choice after time has passed, the next step is to learn if the name is already in use.

A Google search is usually a good place to start. If Google doesn't return a link with your ideal business name, next check for registered trademarks at www.uspto.gov/trademarks/process/search/.

If you don't find your prospective name registered as a trademark, then do a business name search in your state. Do this by searching the phrase "business name availability (your state's name)." Usually, this search will bring up your state's business filings bureau where you can learn if anyone else is already using the name you have in mind.

After you have done the research and confirmed that no one else is already using your ideal business name, register it with a business license.

Legal Requirements: Permits and Licenses

For most businesses that don't sell food or alcohol, there are usually four registrations or permits you need to operate legally in the US:

Zoning permit waiver. Most side gigs or small startups will be run from home, which is more than likely in a residential area. Your home probably isn't zoned for doing business. However, you may still be allowed to operate with a zoning waiver as long as your home business activity doesn't draw attention or get complaints from neighbors. Visit your city or county zoning office to learn what's required.

Local business license. Apply at your local county business registration office. Locate yours at: sba.gov/business-guide/launch-your-business/apply-licenses-permits.

State sales tax permit. In the US, except for Alaska, Delaware, Montana, New Hampshire and Oregon, all states require a state sales tax permit for selling products or services in the respective area. To learn where to get a sales tax permit in your state, do an online search for "(your state name) sales tax permit." Usually the state sales tax permit is free. Once you are signed up, the state will send you forms to fill out and return with any sales tax collected. If you will sell at festivals and art and craft shows, most events require a state sales tax permit.

Federal Employer Identification Number (EIN). If your business doesn't have employees, you may not need an EIN. Sole proprietors can use their social security number when reporting business income to the IRS. If you hire others, you'll need the EIN. Apply online at ein-forms-gov.com/.

For starting and registering a business in Canada, see canada.ca/en/services/business/start.html.

For the UK, visit www.gov.uk.

For Australia, start at register.business.gov.au. Also see business.gov.au/registrations/register-for-taxes/tax-registration-for-your-business

Accepting Credit Card Payments

If you sell at trunk shows, home parties, or craft fairs, a mobile credit card reader allows you to accept credit card payments through your mobile phone or notebook.

If you plan to sell on Etsy or Amazon Handmade, you won't need a credit card processor as the site handles transactions and passes on the processing fee to you.

If you have your own website, you will need a credit card processor to handle transactions from online sales.

Does accepting credit cards make a difference? For impulse buys like those at craft shows, the answer is a definite yes. My sales more than doubled when I began accepting cards. I'm not alone. A survey showed 83% of businesses report it increased their sales.

Almost 80% of shoppers prefer using a credit card. Fortunately, technology has made it easy to accept credit cards from just about anywhere. Using a small card reader that plugs into your smartphone and an app from your card processor, you will key in an item, swipe or insert the card, and have the buyer sign with their finger or a stylus pen.

Two popular mobile credit card service providers among craft show vendors are Square at squareup.com and PayPal at paypal.com/us/webapps/mpp/credit_card-reader. Both services allow you to accept credit card payments through your smartphone with no monthly charges and only a per-transaction fee.

Money from a sale minus the fee is deposited directly into your checking account.

Keeping Records / Accounting

Keep records of your sales along with your expenses. The IRS requires businesses to keep records and file income tax, even when you don't show a profit.

There are different ways of keeping records. If you have a smartphone, there are apps like Expensify that allow you to snap photos of your receipts. TaxJar integrates with Etsy shops, making it easy to record sales data. Other accounting tools include: Wave, QuickBooks Self-Employed, GoDaddy Bookkeeping for Etsy Sellers, and Zoho.

Examples of expenses you may be allowed to deduct from your business income include: business-related insurance, show rental fees, bank charges, trade periodicals, advertising, office supplies, utilities, contract labor, salaries, equipment rentals or repairs, depreciation, and the cost of goods sold.

For more tax advantages from your craft business, see my book: *How to Price Crafts and Things You Make to Sell*.

Create a Production Logbook

Keeping a production logbook helps when it comes time to reproduce an item. In my logbook, I include a photo or drawing of each piece with details of material costs, production time, finished dimensions, how well an item sold, and other notes.

Legal and accounting stuff may seem tedious, but doing it right means you can relax and move forward without the worry of future troubles with the government.

Next, let's look at how to brand your messaging to shoppers so you convert more of them from browsers into buyers.

Chapter 3

Branding Your New Business

If you were going on a date and wanted to impress the other person, you would likely take extra steps with grooming and dressing. Likewise, when getting your products ready to market, there are steps for making your line stand out and increase engagement.

This chapter teaches you how to brand your business with your photos, promotional material, and packaging. When selling online or to stores, your presentation has to sell for you.

Promotional material gives you a way to pass along branding cues so customers remember and refer others to you. Branding includes your story and how you message it. It also includes the use of consistent style elements like fonts, colors, and icons that go into your signage, business cards, hangtags, web pages, and more.

Branding Cues

First impressions are often lasting ones, including brand names and logos. Here are the parts that go into building your brand's message. Some of these were also mentioned earlier as being important ways to make your product line stand out from others.

Your Story. People relate to stories. Your story has the potential to pull heartstrings. Mass-manufactured things rarely connect us to actual people behind the products.

Your Business Name. After you've settled on the name you intend to use, place it throughout your promotional material.

Your Authenticity. Large companies have a problem conveying authenticity. Corporations don't have souls. As a small business, if you are authentic, that's your brand. No one else is like you. All of your choices around logos, fonts, colors, and images can reflect your personality.

Images. Images tell stories. They deliver visuals when you are marketing online and for your display when you are at art or craft shows. You need: product-only images with a white background for online store listings, how-it's-made images, how-it's-used images if needed, lifestyle images showing people enjoying your item, jury images when applying to arts and crafts fairs, and pictures of you to accompany your artist's story.

Your Logo. A logo is a small visual that expresses a feeling you want to convey to shoppers. Later in this chapter, you will find where you can get free templates or hire professional graphic designers.

Your Elevator Pitch. In a few brief sentences (30 seconds or less to say) what does your product promise customers?

Fonts and Colors. Consistency is part of good branding. Choose fonts and colors and use those same ones on all your printed materials and website content.

Your Contact Information. Every message you send or promote through should contain information on how people can easily reach you, including your website, phone number, e-mail, and address.

When thinking about how to design your brand's look and feel, get inspired by checking out how successful sellers brand their business.

Head over to <u>Craftcount.com</u> and choose the category closest to your product line. Craftcount displays the top-selling Etsy shops.

Also, check out Amazon bestsellers by category at <u>https://www.amazon.com/Handmade</u>/. Starting in the "Handmade" category, drill down into the subcategories closest to yours and Amazon will show you the top sellers in those niches.

Getting Great Photos

Great photos convert online shoppers into buyers. And posters with images of people using or holding your product can boost sales at art and craft fairs.

The six types of product images that can help your sales:

1. **Product-only images with a white background** for online store listings (required when selling on Amazon). Etsy images don't have to have a white background, but studies show they improve online sales.

2. **How-it's-made images**. Pictures of you making your products. Tell your story through photos.

3. **Step-by-step instructional images** where a person in the photo shows how to use a product, if applicable.

4. **Lifestyle images** showing people in real-life poses enjoying your item. If you can get them, use images of real customers (who have given permission) using your products.

5. **Jury images** to submit when applying to arts and crafts fairs.

6. **Pictures of you** to accompany your artist's story in your promotional materials and your social media profiles.

Learning Photography

If your work is one-of-a-kind pieces, you will be taking a lot of photos. But even if you make reproducible items, you need to photograph an object from different angles. Learn photography or brush up on your skills at the following sites:

* join.shawacademy.com/online-photography-course
* alison.com/tag/photography
* youtube.com/user/tutvid/playlists
* bit.ly/PHLearnVids (Photoshop tutorials)

Finding photographers

Commercial product photographers can cost hundreds or even thousands of dollars. Though you get great pics, you may not have the funds to invest so much money starting out. There are cheaper alternatives:

- Ask a friend who's photos you admire to take pictures of your work. Even if you have to pay them, it's worth the money to get better images. If you get photos from a friend, have a consent form that grants you the copyright license to use the photos wherever you need to.
- At Fiverr.com I searched for "product photography" and found affordable rates. Copyright is included in the fees. Look for providers with positive reviews and many completed gigs. I only work with those who have received multiple five-star ratings.
- Another source for finding photographers is Etsy.com. Type in the search bar "product photography" for thousands of results. Most services are for product images only, not models. If your product needs a model, expect to pay more.
- Also search for "mockup" on Etsy for thousands of examples of products in lifestyle settings.
- CreativeMarket.com and DesignCuts.com offer a vast collection of mockups for simulating your product image in a lifestyle setting.
- For more craft photography tips, see the resources at: handmadeology.com/big-list-of-product-photography-tips/ and the book *Photographing Arts, Crafts & Collectibles* by Steve Meltzer.

Types of Promotional Materials

Once you have your branding cues created and available, you can repurpose them again and again into your promotional messaging using:

Videos. Tell your artist's story with video. Over 70% (and rising) of shoppers say video influenced their purchases. Over 90% of watchers are likely to remember a call to action on a video. Etsy, Amazon, and most social sites support and encourage product videos to increase sales.

Business cards are among the entrepreneur's cheapest yet most useful tools. Your business card provides all your contact information.

Hangtags. Every piece you sell should have a hanging tag that gives details about your product: the way you made it, simple instructions for product care when appropriate, and something like the words "handcrafted by" your name.

Thank You cards. With every sale, including a signed Thank You card adds a personal touch that customers will appreciate because so many sellers neglect to do it. Include your logo and contact info on the back. When I pack an online order to send out, I place a Thank You card with a coupon for a discount off the customer's next order.

Packaging. Packaging is another opportunity for branding and messaging. Use (and let customers know that you use): biodegradable packaging, upcycled corrugated cardboard, recycled paper, or other biodegradable organic materials.

Signs and banners. If you do craft shows, expos, or trunk shows, use signs and banners. Many office supply stores can take your PDF file and create a sign with foam board backing, lamination and grommet holes for hanging for a reasonable price. Include your business name, a brief blurb or positive review quote, and your website address on your signs.

Postcards make low-cost reminders to mail to previous customers. Cards can include an eye-catching image on one side and marketing message, name, address, and website on the other side. Postcards can help sell new products and close-outs. Mail cards periodically to your customer list. Send out invitational notecards to your mailing list whenever you will be back in their area to do a show or home party. One side of the card has your latest catchy image. Since there's no envelope to decide about opening, customers have to see your photo.

Your voice mail message. If you don't always answer your phone, your voice mail message can communicate a marketing message. Include your website address and perhaps information about an upcoming craft show where you will be displaying. It means updating your message regularly if you do a lot of shows, but it creates the impression of someone who is busy selling.

Checks, return address labels, sales receipts, gift certificates, order forms, and sticker labels provide more opportunities to add a logo, website and promo blurb about what you do. When I accept credit cards at art and craft shows, the customer receives an e-mail or text receipt that includes my business name, a photo of me, and contact information so they can easily remember who they made the purchase from.

Graphic Design Providers

Good design in your marketing materials is as important as good product images. Get started with easy-to-use templates:

- Canva.com
- GetStencil.com
- Snappa.com
- Fotor.com
- DesignBold.com

If you don't want to design your own materials, hire graphic designers to do it for you at:

- CreativeMarket.com
- MockupEditor.com
- DesignHill.com
- CrowdSpring.com
- Fiverr.com
- HatchWise.com (logos)
- Etsy.com Search for "logo design" or "banner design" or "etsy shop makeover"

Printing Services
- VistaPrint.com
- GotPrint.com
- Moo.com
- Printique.com

Preparing your small business for prime time has hopefully gotten you excited about launching your product line. Next in our steps of getting ready for the marketplace, we need to price your crafts so you make a profit. The next chapter reveals the pricing formula for selling in retail or wholesale and online and off.

CHAPTER 4

How to Price Wood Crafts

This chapter teaches you how to price your wood crafts so you make a healthy and fair profit. Knowing your profit margins guides your choices in where and what you will sell and how you grow your business.

What you will learn:
- Understanding retail and wholesale pricing
- Discovering how much shoppers will pay
- How much it costs you to make an item
- The pricing formula
- Your profit margin
- Pricing one-of-a-kind work

Understanding Retail and Wholesale Pricing

You may sell your handmade pieces in several markets like on Etsy or Amazon, in gift shops, to interior designers, at craft shows and expos, through galleries, or even mail-order catalogs. These markets fall into one of two categories: retail or wholesale. This section describes the different approaches for pricing in each category.

Retail pricing is the amount you ask for a piece when you are selling direct to a customer. Examples of places you might sell retail include art and craft shows, festivals, online through a website, home parties, or from your own studio.

Wholesale pricing is the amount you charge for items you sell to someone else who resells your products to their customers. For instance, stores, galleries, interior designers, and catalogs like Sundance Catalog are wholesale markets. Stores price items two to two-and-a-half times what they pay for them.

If you plan to grow your business by selling to stores, knowing your costs and your prices tells you if you can afford to sell wholesale. Imagine having fifty or more stores around the country showing your items five to seven days a week.

There's no definitive answer to whether wholesale or retail is a better business model. I know makers who will not do craft shows, choosing instead to work from home. I know others who only do shows or sell online and never wholesale. And there are other sellers like me who do both.

How Much Will Shoppers Pay?

The question almost every new maker asks is, "How much should I charge for my work?" An even more important question is, "How much will shoppers pay?"

You don't want to lose money by asking only enough to get back your costs when customers will gladly pay higher prices.

You may find the average market price for an item is higher at one place than it is for similar work in a different market(s). For example, a set of wood letters may sell on Etsy at one price, at craft fairs at a different price, and in stores for a higher price.

Below are the major e-commerce sites where you can survey prices for handmade items with a sales history. We don't want all product listings. We want those that have a sales history, because it provides evidence that the item's price was in line with buyer expectations.

www.etsyrank.com. EtsyRank (mentioned in Chapter 1) is a subscription service that lets you quickly assess competition of your keywords and products. Type in words closely describing your item and EtsyRank will return related keywords and the top sellers and their prices.

www.marmalead.com. Marmalead, like Etsyrank, is a subscription service providing similar analytics of Etsy keywords, sales, and prices.

www.craftcount.com. On craftcount.com, you can quickly view the top sellers on Etsy by category. Clicking on the seller's link brings up their store. It's a safe bet that they have found good price points because of their high sales volume.

www.ebay.com. On the left side of the page, under "categories", select "crafts", then look for and click on "handcrafted & finished pieces." Then look for "preferences" and choose "completed listings." On the right side of the results page are completed auction listings of products. Sort the listings by choosing "price: highest first." Look for: (1) products that are selling, (2) number of bids—this shows whether people are eager to buy these crafts, (3) price—shows the highest bid or how much people will pay.

www.sundancecatalog.com. Sundance Catalog is among the most popular mail-order catalogs featuring handmade items. They mail copies to millions of shoppers. Unfortunately, for the craft artist, catalogs want items priced that they can mark up at least four times.

www.artfulhome.com. If you want to sell to interior designers, this is a impressive site to check prices on. Some pieces listed here sell for thousands of dollars.

www.faire.com. A major site allowing handmakers a way to offer their product lines to wholesale buyers. To help store buyers, Faire also shows what items are bestsellers or in their words, products "flying off the shelf."

www.merchantwords.com. MerchantWords (described earlier) can pull sales data from Amazon Handmade buyers. For insights into average market prices, look for product listings (of items like yours) with reviews. The more reviews, the more an item has sold, therefore the price must be right.

www.qvc.com. In the search box, type in a craft item similar to what you make like "birdhouse," "cutting board," "ornament," "decor idea," or just type in "handmade". Note the prices the items sell for. QVC buys in quantity and then resells stuff at a marked up price. QVC has been around on TV since 1986 and are very good at buying items that sell.

Knowing what shoppers are used to paying for craft items like yours, you next need to know your costs for making them.

Cost of Goods or Production Cost

* * *

There are several issues to consider when estimating costs of raw lumber:

- You usually have scraps left after a project is complete. Though you may be able to make small craft items from the leftovers, you want to get paid back for the total cost of wood needed for the main project.
- When buying wood, you don't always end up with perfect boards, unless you carefully pick them out yourself. And even then, you sometimes miss a flaw or board that isn't straight. When figuring material costs, account for extra pieces of wood in case of mistakes. Over time, you'll come up with an average amount of overage you need to buy per project.
- It will cost you gas and time to go and pick up supplies from your lumber yard. Figure in your cost of travel.

* * *

Cost of goods is what you spend to produce the products you sell. Cost of goods includes all material, labor, and overhead costs.

Let's use wind chimes as an example, because they are a steady seller at craft shows and online. "Wind chimes" was searched for over 28,800 times in a recent month on Etsy.

Materials Cost

Your materials include wood, glue, hinges, accessories, and all other supplies needed to complete a project. As an example, say you make wind chimes from wood and recycled materials. For our example, let's say your total materials cost for one set of chimes is $9:

Labor Cost

Cost of labor is the dollar value of the time needed to gather, prepare and produce an item. The cost of labor will be the hourly wage you pay yourself or the wages you pay others as employees or independent contractors.

How much is your time worth? This is something you have to decide, but I wouldn't start lower than $20 per hour.

If you can sell items at a price that would pay you $30, $35, or more per hour, you can profitably hire others at a lower rate (like $15 per hour) to help produce your pieces when sales justify outsourcing labor.

Continuing with the example of the wind chimes, let's say you decided that you value your labor at $20 per hour.

Time to arrange materials before assembly: 2 minutes
Time to assemble one set of chimes: 13 minutes
Cost of labor: .25 hours (15 minutes) x $20 per hour = $5

Note: when you make a piece for the first time, your labor time will be longer. After making several, you will have learned ways to cut the production time. With practice, you'll arrive at the true cost of your labor.

Cost of materials for the wind chimes is $9 and cost of labor is $5, bringing your costs to $14. We now need to account for another, often overlooked cost of doing business commonly known as overhead.

Overhead Cost

Overhead refers to expenses you pay to operate your business day-to-day, even if you work from home. Overhead is also referred to as fixed costs because these expenses remain in a predictable range throughout the year, regardless of how much you sell.

Examples of overhead include: business licenses, rent, utilities, phone, insurance, advertising, office supplies, cleaning supplies, professional dues, and so on.

Calculating all those costs would take time. More established businesses will do the due diligence, but an easy shortcut for a home business is to figure 25 percent of the total of your materials and labor costs to arrive at a number that approximates your overhead.

Adding estimated overhead costs for wind chimes:
$5 labor + $9 materials = $14
$14 x 25% estimated overhead = $3.50

Total production cost for wind chimes:
$14 + $3.5 = $17.50

The Pricing Formula

As you can see in the example above, the total of labor, materials and overhead for making one wind chimes is $17.50. This is the amount we have to recover to break even. But $17.50 isn't necessarily what you would price your wind chimes at.

Go back to the research you did earlier to learn the average market price for wind chimes. You may find those like yours sell on Etsy or Amazon or at crafts fairs for an average price of $20 or more. Since that's a price that shoppers are used to seeing, you would be in line to price yours at least $20. If you use recycled materials, you can ask a little more, even though your costs are lower. Multiple surveys report that shoppers will pay more to own sustainably produced items (source: Fortune.com.)

Calculating Wholesale Prices

Let's say wind chimes like yours sell in stores for $38. That means they paid $19 or less to the seller. Shops mark up items two to two and half times to arrive at their retail price.

Your break-even cost is $17.50. As long as your wholesale price to stores doesn't drop below $17.50, you can make money selling wholesale.

But what if your break-even cost had been higher, like $20. In a case like that, one needs to:

* Lower material or labor costs, and / or

* Enhance the perceived value of the wind chimes so the store owner will bump up the retail, or

* Choose different items to make that are profitable.

What's Your Profit Margin?

One of the most important things to learn early on in your business is your profit margin. This amount is the difference between your cost of goods and your asking price.

If your cost of goods is $17.50 and your retail price is $35, your gross profit is $17.50. If you are selling online, that $17.50 gets eaten into by seller fees. You might actually end up with more like $13 or $14.

If you sell at craft shows, your net profit per piece will be even less because you have travel expenses, show rental fees, food, supplies, etc.

Knowing profit margins enables you to make choices for growth by telling you:

- If you can afford to hire help with production, which will allow you to produce more inventory.
- How much money you can spend on ads.
- If you can profitably sell wholesale to stores where you can scale up your business by adding more and more accounts.
- If you can afford to offer free shipping, which will increase your sales.

Pricing One-of-a-Kind Items

Pricing one-of-a-kind products differs from pricing a product line you make over and over. It's more challenging to price unique items because the maker uses different materials for every piece and may not be able to consistently predict how long it takes to complete a new project.

The good news is that by their nature, one-of-a-kind objects are scarce. People want things that are rare or difficult to get. When you emphasize that a specific piece is the only one of its kind, you immediately raise its value.

Pricing by the Square Foot

A woodworker friend who was well connected with wealthy home owners in New Mexico asked me to make woven wall screens. The question became how to quote prices for making screens which would vary according to the home owner's needs. The customer may want a set of 4' x 8' screens, 2' x 5' or some other size.

The wood I used came from salt cedar cuttings; the color resembles beautiful mahogany. Salt cedar is an unwanted invader crop in New Mexico and Arizona. I can spend time going to where it grows and cut as much as I want for free, or I can buy the canes in bundles. For this example, let's say I am buying bundles. One bundle will cost me $20, enough for one 3' x 6' screen. We'll use that size screen for a pricing-by-the-foot example.

It takes an average of 75 minutes to cut the canes, weave them into a screen, and add draw string clutches to make it function like a window screen one can raise and lower.

If I figure my labor at $30 per hour, one screen comes to $37.50 in labor costs.

Other materials include $10 in fibers, clutches, thread, and accessories. Adding the cost of the cane, my total material cost is $30 per screen.

Labor and materials come to $67.50. I also want to recover any overhead (estimating at 25% of my other costs), so I multiply $67.50 x 25% to cover indirect expenses and get $16.88.

Total production cost of one of my screens looks like this:

Materials: $30
Labor: $37.50
Overhead: $16.88
Total: $84.38

Next, I double my costs of goods as if I were a store buying from a supplier. This ensures a healthy profit:

$$\$84.38 \times 2 = \$168.76$$

I need a reliable "per square foot price" I can quote a customer asking about a custom-sized piece. The square footage of my finished 3' x 6' screen comes to 18 square feet. I divide the amount I arrived at above by the square footage:

$$\$168.76 \div 18 = \$9.38$$

I round this number up to $10 per square foot to make it easier when talking with a customer. Confident that my costs are covered and I am making a profit, I can approach interior designers about selling my screens to their clients. They would add their own commission fee to my $10 per foot price.

If you are working with interior designers, architects, builders, or real estate agents, ask for feedback about your price per square foot. It may be your price is low compared to others in the market. If so, learn the average price for work similar to yours and raise your price accordingly.

Scarce Items Command Higher Prices

One-of-a-kind pieces are immediately more valuable and deserving of higher prices because of the scarcity factor. Shoppers desire a singular piece because it is special. Owning it gives exclusivity—like being a member of a VIP club.

In his bestselling book *Influence, The Psychology of Persuasion*, Robert Cialdini, Ph.D., the author says we are attracted to things when their availability is limited. Studies show we are more likely to buy something if we think it is the last one or the only one of its kind.

What Others Charge

It may not be easy to find examples in the market of work like yours since one-of-a-kind means . . . well, not-like-anything-else. If you can find pieces like yours, then you aren't making one-of-a-kind items.

When searching Etsy for "one of a kind" (including the quote marks) I found over 30,000 listings. In the category of Handmade on Amazon, only 2,000 items.

One-of-a-kinders have to bend their imaginations when assessing work that comes close to their own. Is this piece like mine?

If you can't find work similar to yours, don't worry. Calculate your costs (labor and materials) and multiply by four. Put your pieces on the market and observe how shoppers react.

Prices range dramatically. For example, one-of-a-kind handmade, collectible wood dolls sell from $8,300 to $11,000 according to Dollery.com.

Artfulhome.com lists one-of-a-kind pieces in the furniture category at prices ranging from $395 to $22,000.

As Your Brand Grows, So Can Your Prices

Being able to sell one-of-a-kind items at high prices relies on accumulating a list of paying customers, and eventually your reputation as an artisan.

There's no formula for matching your reputation to your prices, but you can look to successful artists as examples of what's possible. What do we mean by successful? When an artist or artisan gets publicity for their work again and again, their personal brand is succeeding.

Ask Galleries

Galleries showcase one-of-a-kind pieces. Talking with an established gallery's manager can help you determine a piece's price because they know their clientele over time and know what their customers will pay.

Gallery owners want sales. A major consideration in pricing art or one-of-a-kind pieces is the reputation of the artist. A newer artisan's work may not get the same treatment or even accepted into a gallery.

Visit galleries that represent work something like yours. The gallery manager may be willing to show you the resumes of their other artisans. Looking at the background of other artists and noting the prices asked for their work, you can better estimate what you should be charging. Remember that the gallery is adding a markup to all work shown, probably around 100%.

When presenting your work to a gallery or dealer, discuss retail prices. The gallery owner will advise you based on their experience. Say you've created a wood sculpture for a gallery who recommends a retail price of $2,000. After the item sells, you would receive $1,000, which is a 50/50 split with the gallery.

When I first opened my gallery/shop's doors, I didn't have much inventory from local artists and artisans. I temporarily stocked my displays with handmade pieces from other countries. Nice-looking stuff I could buy wholesale.

My cost for this merchandise was low. I priced them at twice my cost and put them on display. Despite their attractiveness, nothing sold. So I raised prices, thinking shoppers considered the items were too cheap to be handmade. I raised prices twice again before the pieces started selling.

* * *

Woodworking usually involves an investment in tools. When you buy an expensive piece of equipment to be used in crafting your products, it can be a business deduction. How you deduct equipment costs is a matter to discuss with an accountant, as tax law changes almost yearly.

* * *

With all the preparations you have done so far, you are ready to map out where, when, and how you will get your crafts in front of buyers. The next chapter shows you how to schedule your marketing action steps.

CHAPTER 5

Your Marketing Plan

With so many directions to go in, it helps to map out your promotional actions day by day, using a marketing calendar or daily planner. With a map and a schedule, you never have to wonder what to do next.

Start with the possibilities extracted from this book. They won't all be appropriate for you, but circle those that are so you can add them to your calendar or planner. You will develop your own ideas as you grow in experience. Add your tactics to the list and to your calendar.

If you enjoy being on the road, art and craft shows provide opportunities to travel and sell your work. If you prefer staying at home, think about selling online, or only traveling now and then to approach galleries or shops appropriate for what you make.

Some artisans concentrate on one marketing venue and get good there. Others diversify and sell wholesale, retail, and take on commission work. The right model is the one that works for you.

* * * * * *

What Is Marketing?

The word marketing is often used interchangeably with advertising. Though advertising is a marketing tactic, it is only one of many. Not all marketing costs money. Here's what marketing is; it is every communication you make about your product, yourself, or your products. It's how you describe what you do, how you dress, your business card, your product packaging, the colors you choose for your logo, and a lot more.

* * * * * *

Marketing Actions

The following suggested actions, grouped by topics, are available as a checklist you can add your own ideas to. This list is a summary for reference. The ideas are explained more fully throughout this book. Download my list of 100 marketing tactics for handmakers at: https://craftmarketer.com/book-resources/

MAKING PRODUCTS
Research products in demand
Write your story
Make quality products
Create products using themes
Personalize products

PHOTOS & VIDEOS
Take lots of attractive photos
Product images with white background for Amazon
How-it's-made images & videos
How-it's-used images & videos
Lifestyle images
Jury images for art & craft shows
Headshot images of you

BIZ STARTUP
Choose a catchy business name
Register for a business license
Get set up to accept credit cards
Set up accounting system

PRE-MARKETING
Find your authentic voice
Design logo
Elevator pitch
Choose your fonts and colors
Add your contact info
Business cards
Hangtags
Thank you cards
Signs and banners for events
Postcards
Voice mail message
Branding on all stationery

PRICING
Average prices for similar work?
Your production cost
Your profit margin
Can you lower your costs?

SELL AT EVENTS
Research art and craft shows, events
Apply to shows
Build attractive display
Get pop-up tent
Make a checklist for doing shows

SEO - SEARCH ENGINE OPTIMIZATION
Use EtsyRank or MerchantWords to find keywords
Use keywords in social posts
Use keywords in product listings
Get inbound links

SELL ON ETSY
Set up new Etsy shop, or
Get critique of Etsy shop
List products
Keywords in title, tags, descriptions

Add 10 images per listing
Connect Etsy to social media
Test Etsy ads
Increase number of listings
Market Etsy store offline
Offer free shipping if possible

ALTERNATIVES TO ETSY
List on Amazon Handmade
List on other Etsy alternatives
Set up your own domain site
WordPress plugin for Etsy Store
Test ads on social media sites

SOCIAL MEDIA
Post at least once a day or more
Post with video for engagement
Posts: educate, entertain, inspire
Post links to your products
Schedule posting using apps
Research popular hashtags
Post on Facebook
Post to Instagram
Pin to Pinterest boards
Aim at getting social followers' e-mails

SELL WHOLESALE
Determine production capacity
Costs = 25% or less of the retail price
Professional presentation
Find store buyers using LinkedIn
List on Houzz and ArtfulHome
Offer online ordering for stores

FREE PUBLICITY
Prepare online media kit
Identify influencers with Heepsy
USNPL lists newspaper writers

Create brief pitch to media
Link to full press release

CUSTOMER MAILING LIST
Set up e-mail management app like Aweber or Mailchimp
Ask customers to give e-mail
Schedule follow-up calendar

MISCELLANEOUS
Track and measure all actions
Listen to what shoppers tell you
Answer all inquiries quickly
Personalize communications
Treat customers fabulously
Make stuff you love making
Daily Planner / Marketing Calendar

After you identify which action steps you want to work with, use a calendar to organize and schedule them. A planner / marketing calendar protects you from getting lost by mapping a direction. It shows you the big picture.

Your calendar helps you avoid costly shotgun marketing and engage in laser-focused, profitable actions you can track and measure.

Now that you have a plan and a calendar of steps to take, you may be wondering about the fastest way to start making sales. For most sellers that's craft shows, expos, and events, described next.

CHAPTER 6

Selling at Craft Shows, Expos, and Events

Craft fairs, festivals, and consumer expos attract thousands of shoppers who buy handmade items. Craft shows are a great venue for testing your products to learn how shoppers react. Events can also be a fast way to put cash in your wallet.

I like shows and events, because they are a short-term commitment. You can do one or two, measure how shoppers react to your product line, and if you make sales, go on to do more events as it suits you.

Selling at shows has challenges. Events can be physically and energetically taxing. At a busy show, you may talk to hundreds of shoppers about your products and your process.

With so many events happening year round, it's important to choose the right ones for your work. The better-attended shows require vendors to pay for booth rental fees six months or longer in advance of the event. The top shows are highly competitive because they historically perform well for sellers.

Discover if selling at fairs and events is for you. Here we cover:

- Types of events
- Where to find events
- How much shows cost you
- How much you can earn
- How to apply
- Displaying your products
- More tips for having great shows

Types of Events

Events and shows that hand-makers display their work at include:

Art and craft shows. Art and craft shows can be juried or not. Juried means you apply with images of your work and judges accept or reject your application. Jurying (ideally) weeds out vendors selling imported products that are not handmade.

Juried shows are often annual events with a history of good attendance. Examples of annual juried art and craft shows that draw hundreds of thousands of visitors include: Plaza Art Fair in Kansas City; Rio Grande Arts and Crafts Fair Balloon Festival in Albuquerque; One-of-a-Kind Holiday Show in Chicago; Tempe Festival of the Arts in the Phoenix area; and Bayou City Art Festival in Houston.

Renaissance fairs. These outdoor events include vendors of arts and crafts booths as a part of a total entertainment package featuring a medieval theme.

A variety of food, drink, jugglers, jousters, knights and fair maidens abound at these festivals. Some popular renaissance shows run each weekend from one to two months. Vendors commit to a long-term booth and decorate with a medieval theme.

Examples: Arizona Renaissance Festival held weekends from early February to late March in Gold Canyon, AZ; Sherwood Forest Faire held from early February to early March in McDade, TX; Florida Renaissance Festival in February and March in Deerfield Beach, FL; and Minnesota Renaissance Festival held weekends from mid-August until end-September in Shakopee, MN.

High-end flea markets. If you make low-priced items like earrings, bracelets, etc., consider trying a popular flea market if there's one local to you. One of the most well-known is First Monday in Canton, Texas, attracting over 250,000 visitors each month.

Be Wary of...

After years of displaying at different kinds of events, both winners and losers, I urge caution when considering:

First-time events. Avoid events that are new. First-time shows have not built a following so attendance can be poor to non-existent.

Be highly suspicious of **show promoters who approach you at a show** attempting to sell you on applying to their upcoming event. They will tell you how great their show is and how their vendors are all happy with their sales. Reality check. If their show was as good as they make it out to be, they wouldn't need to look for vendors. The better shows always get more applicants than there are available booth spaces.

Music festivals. Music festivals draw huge crowds, but they are mostly there for the partying. However, some makers do sell at these events. If there is a local annual music festival, walk through it and observe how many people are visiting the craft vendor booths. If it looks like makers are selling, the event may be worth trying next year.

Finding Events

How do you find the good craft shows, festivals and expos where you can expect decent sales? Find events (sometimes with vendor reviews) online at:
- zapplication.org
- art-linx.com
- artfaircalendar.com
- festivalnet.com

Questions to Answer before Applying for Events

* Is the show well known? How many years has it been held?

* Does the promoter advertise in the newspapers, on the radio, billboards, or TV? Better shows are well-promoted each year. The public knows about them and returns faithfully to see what's new.

* How many booth spaces are available? A show with 500 booths will draw bigger crowds than a show with only fifty.

* What is the booth rental fee? Is there an extra fee for corner spaces? Usually there is because corners are better selling locations.

* Is there a jury fee? Popular shows charge a separate fee just for applying. The application fee isn't returned if you are rejected, nor is it deducted from your booth fee if you are accepted.

* What size spaces are available? The typical size is 10' x 10' and that is the most common pop-up canopy tent size available.

* Is the event restricted to handmade items?

* Is the show outdoors or inside? If outdoors, what has the weather historically been like at that time of year?

* If the show is outdoors, is it held on streets, sidewalks, parking lots, or a grassy area? Most streets are not level, requiring you to adjust your booth display.

* What are the hours of the event? Most shows require someone to be in your booth throughout the show hours.

* Is booth setup allowed the day before? If you get into a show where this is the case, take advantage of it.

* How is vendor loading and unloading organized?

* How far away is vendor parking?

* What are the security arrangements? Well-organized outdoor events provide security overnight. When you purchase your pop-up tent, get one with side panels so you can zip up the walls.

What Shows Cost

Show expenses include:

* Jury application fees for the more competitive events (non-refundable even if you are not accepted)

* Booth space rental (usually 10' x 10')

* Travel costs: gas, motel, meals, parking fees

* Your display (grid walls or artist pro-panels, tables)

* Pop-up canopy with side walls

* Weights (to keep your tent from blowing away)

* Mobile credit card processing (Squareup.com doesn't charge a monthly fee; you only pay a fee per sale.)

Vendor rental fees at art and craft shows range from $50 a day to $1,000+ for a weekend. Local events, like those sponsored by a high school, church or community center, can be inexpensive and easier to get accepted in. Small local events will cost less because you won't have to spend money on travel.

Big-city, popular juried shows charge higher booth-rental fees. They get more applicants than there are available spaces. The sales potential of well-attended shows can be good (but not guaranteed) so traveling to a neighboring state may be worth the added costs.

How Much Can You Earn?

Unfortunately, it's impossible to estimate your potential earnings from shows without doing them and measuring the results for yourself.

I've been in shows where I sold nothing. When this happens, I don't go back the next year. On the other end of the spectrum, one event (Tempe Festival of the Arts) brought in over $10,000 in sales over a three-day period. I returned to the show year after year with significant results but did not reach that number again. (I originally found the Tempe Festival by googling "top craft shows in the US").

Other sellers I met at different shows told me they did not do well at Tempe and would never go back. If I had talked to them before I experienced my fantastic weekend, I might never have tried it. You cannot rely on what I or other vendors tell you about their earnings from shows. Their success or disappointment doesn't prove the same event will perform similarly for your product line. Sure, it's an indicator, but you can only really know from doing the show yourself.

The best advice I can give you about events is to walk through a show you think might be good for your work and observe how busy the other vendors are. If they are actively selling, then consider applying for the event the following year.

How to Apply

Most shows and fairs require vendors to fill out an application, either online or via a mailed-in form. Zapplication.org lets you apply to and pay for multiple shows from one website. For the more competitive shows, vendor applications are often due six months to a year before the actual show date.

Jury Images

If applying for the more competitive events, it may be worth the investment to hire a photographer experienced in art or craft images for juried shows. If you can't afford a photographer and have to take your own photos, see the examples at: http://bermangraphics.com/digital-jury-resources/fixing-jury-images.htm.

Booth Location

You can't always choose your booth location, but, when possible, take advantage of the opportunity. If you have exhibited at an event in the past, managers may give you the same location you had before or at least give your booth preference a higher priority.

Corner locations (extra fee) can be better because they allow you to open up to traffic flow from two sides.

Getting a booth space near a main walkway close to the show's main entrance will probably be a better location than at the back of the event. Though at well-attended shows, there are no bad locations.

Avoid getting a space near food vendors or entertainment. Food is the top seller at shows and not only are you competing for attention, you must deal with junk food being carried in and around your work. Noise from the entertainment can prevent you from being able to talk to your customers pleasantly. If you don't like your allotted space, ask the show manager before you set up if you can move.

Displaying Your Products

Your booth should be inviting for customers to enter. Build your display at home first, and play with variations of how the arrangement looks with your pieces displayed.

Design the layout of your booth to be flexible. Build it so you can set up at least two ways:

- One side opens to the public. There are booths on three sides of yours.
- Corner space with two sides open for visitor traffic coming from two directions.

There are lots of possibilities for setting up your display and you can keep trying various set ups until you find one customers seem happy with.

For ideas for booth displays, see:

- pinterest.com/lifethriftylane/craft-show-display-ideas/
- pinterest.com/junqdiva/diy-craft-show-display-and-set-up-ideas/
- pinterest.com/dillydally/craft-show-booth-inspiration/

Pop-Up Canopy Tent

* For outdoor events, you need protection from sun and weather. A pop-up canopy will adequately protect you and your pieces.

* Physical safety of your customers, fellow vendors, and your merchandise should be a priority in constructing your booth. Frame and covers should be sturdy enough to withstand high winds, rain, and large crowds.

* Bring weights to attach to your pop-up tent. Weights keep your tent from blowing into your neighbor's display.

* White tarps work best with pop-up tents. Colored tarps cast a hue on your merchandise.

* Get a pop-up tent you can quickly set up and easily break down for transport. You want to be able to quickly set up your tent and break it down at the end of the event.

* KD canopy and EZ Up have been making pop-up tents for art and craft fairs for many years. Check Craigslist or eBay for deals. Search for "canopy tent" or "ez up tent" or "pop-up tent".

More Tips for Successful Shows

* Show up to events early. You never know how setup will go with many vendors arriving at the same time—all in a hurry to get their displays up.

* Bring a small folding table to carry out sales transactions. This will be where the customer can comfortably write a check or sign for a credit card sale. Keep extra pens around.

* Make it easy for customers to buy. Have everything you need to complete a sale, including: receipt book, brochures, business cards, price lists, and bags or boxes for packaging sales.

* Have a receipt book for customers who want a written receipt. Writing a receipt also makes an excuse to ask the customer to be on your mailing list.

* Even when someone doesn't buy, but has spent time asking you questions, let them know you have a mailing list that offers specials now and then.

* Have a supply of artist statements, bookmarks, business cards or postcards about you and your work to give with each sale or inquiry.

* For indoor events, consider buying a carpet remnant or rug for your booth. It looks good and gives you and your customers some relief from concrete floors.

* Make price signs or price tags. You will tire of answering the question, "How much is it?"

* For makers of wearables, wear something you have made; be a walking ad for your work.

* If you have won competitions, post your awards.

* Bring your own food. It lessens your time away from your booth during the busy part of the day.

* Keep notes about shows by name, city, travel distance, costs, crowd size, weather, parking, layout, sales, and other notes to yourself.

* Shows can be both exciting and demanding. Hundreds, possibly thousands of potential customers come by your booth,

many of whom will look at your work and talk to you briefly. It helps if a friend or family member can assist you. Setting up the booth and handling sales goes easier with two people.

Events let you meet people, make sales, and add new names to your customer list. Not everyone will buy at an event, but they may take your card or agree to be on your mailing list.

At almost every event I display at, within days afterwards, I get orders on my Etsy store from someone who saw my pieces at the show but for whatever reason did not buy then.

Though meeting customers at events is probably the fastest way to market your products—cool handmade stuff practically sells itself—you may prefer to stay home and sell online. The coming chapters give you tools and resources for growing an e-commerce business. The first step is understanding SEO or Search Engine Optimization.

CHAPTER 7

SEO – How Buyers Search Online

SEO—or search engine optimization—refers to using techniques to improve a web page's likelihood of showing up in search results for specific search terms or keywords. What does this have to do with making and selling wood crafts?

If your product listing, blog post or YouTube video shows up on the first page for a search, it brings you free, organic traffic. There aren't many ways to market for free, but SEO is probably the closest to free you will find.

When you think of search engines, Google, Bing, or Yahoo may come to mind. But Etsy, Amazon, and eBay are also search engines, besides being huge marketplaces with shopping carts.

The factors that go into how e-commerce search engines rank one page over another for specific keyword searches change frequently as sites develop toward creating relevant results for users. But there are elements that consistently influence search rankings, which you will discover in the following topics:

- Finding search terms buyers use
- Keyword tools

Search is powerful. It has driven the boom of e-commerce both through computers and more and more on mobile devices. Eighty-seven percent of people using a smartphone search online at least once a day.

People search online for solutions to their problems. They search for opportunities. They search for entertainment. They search to learn. More important to you, they search for handmade products to buy for themselves or as gifts.

You have probably come across the following words: tags, keywords, and search terms. For our purposes, they refer to the same thing. They are the words and phrases people type in a search bar to find what they need online.

Search Terms Buyers Use

In order for your product pages to show up in search results, you must include popular and relevant search terms used by shoppers. If you don't use popular search terms on your pages, for the most part, your items won't get found.

Because SEO is technical and often confusing, the simplest way to explain how SEO works is to show you an example. Let's say I make cutting boards. I am not sure how buyers search for items like mine, so I need a keyword research tool. In Chapter 1, we learned about a tool for Etsy called EtsyRank. Typing in "cutting boards" at EtsyRank.com's keyword tool reveals the following search phrases and number of searches done in a recent 30-day period:

cutting board: 12,080 searches
cutting boards: 3,687 searches
cheese board: 3,421 searches
wood cutting board: 1,495 searches
custom cutting board: 1,447 searches
recipe cutting board: 1,019 searches
maple cutting board: 656 searches
walnut cutting board: 535 searches
bread board: 495 searches
wooden cutting board: 302 searches
bamboo cutting board: 182 searches

The more specific the search term, the higher the probability that the searcher is ready to buy. In the above example, if I make cutting boards from maple wood, I know that there were over 600 searches in a month. That might be enough of a demand to make maple cutting boards.

Assuming I use the phrase "maple cutting board" in my product listing, it would also have a chance of showing up for that phrase and for searches for "cutting board" which is typed in more than 12,000 times a month.

One and two-word tags like "tables" or "chairs" are too broad for you to rank well for. Multi-word phrases are both easier to rank for and more likely to be used by someone ready to buy.

For example, "tray" is a popular search term (over 340,000 searches on Amazon in a recent month) but not very specific. Whereas "wood soap dispenser tray" is a longer search phrase that would be much easier to rank for and more useful for attracting shoppers ready to buy.

Inbound Links to Your Pages

Using popular keywords is an important part of SEO for Etsy, Amazon, and other online stores. But there's another element that can affect your ranking in Google, Yahoo, and Bing search results—inbound links pointing to your product listing pages. An example of an inbound link: a blogger writes a review about one of your products and includes a link to your Etsy store.

Inbound links add authority to your page rankings because they are like votes coming in to tell the search engine that your page is relevant for the text in the link.

If you wanted to rank higher for "wood soap dispenser tray" in Google searches, you would ask some sites to link to you with the link text reading "wood soap dispenser tray." Hidden from the viewer is the actual hyperlink that leads to your page.

But you have to be careful not to go overboard with getting a bunch of inbound links saying the same thing. Google sees this as spam. Instead, you want a variety of inbound link texts, which is more natural in Google's eyes. Some inbound link texts could be your URL. Some could be the phrase for which you want to rank high. And others could be semantically-related phrases or your business name.

Since most wood crafters don't use inbound links as an SEO technique, you won't need many inbound links for specific phrases in order to show up on the first page of Google results. It can take Google a month or two to crawl the web and index those new inbound links, so be patient.

Engagement

Another factor that influences your SEO rankings is the amount and frequency of engagement your page receives from real people. For example, you post a video on your Facebook page with a link to your Etsy store. Your followers click through your link and check out your product pages. That engagement, including how much time a visitor spends, is tracked and measured by Google, which then becomes part of the algorithm that determines how Google will rank your pages for keywords.

Keyword Tools

Etsy provides free "Search Analytics" for sellers with a sales history. This is invaluable if you have been on Etsy for at least a few months and made sales. You'll discover which keywords buyers used to find your product listing. To view, go to your Shop Manager > Marketing > Search analytics. We'll dive more into Etsy in the next chapter.

As described earlier, Etsyrank.com and Marmalead.com are subscription services that make keyword research easier for Etsy sellers. Serious Amazon Handmade sellers may want to consider subscribing to MerchantWords.com. Their tool gives search terms used by real buyers on Amazon.

Are these tools expensive? Subscription fees vary. If you can uncover new search terms that result in increased sales, it could be worth the investment, even if you only use the service for one month. You can export your research, save the search data files, and then cancel your subscription. Search terms are seasonal and can change over time, so come back to the tools every few months.

A note about using Google for research: other sellers use Google for competitive research. So if you use an SEO tool that tells you how many searches on Google were made for a particular phrase, know that those searchers aren't all buyers.

Whatever methods you play with for your keyword research, start off with a list of words and phrases you think best describe your items. Then use the keyword tools to find related terms and phrases used by searchers.

Most services let you export your research results as a spreadsheet file, from which you can sort and arrange the results according to your needs.

SEO may seem intimidating, but even a little research can go a long way to uncovering keyword phrases shoppers are using every day to find products like yours.

Keyword research can also help more people find your blog articles, your posts on Instagram, Pinterest, Facebook, and Twitter, and your product listings on Etsy.

Selling on Etsy requires more than throwing up a bunch of product listings and hoping buyers flock to your online shop. The next chapter prepares you for what you need to know to succeed in this major online marketplace for consumers looking to buy handmade.

CHAPTER 8

Selling on Etsy

E tsy has over 35 million active buyers browsing handmade products from almost two million sellers. Etsy buyers are loyal—81% are repeat customers who account for annual sales exceeding three billion dollars. Etsy's primary market caters to the buy handmade audience.

As a selling platform, Etsy makes it easy to get started for new sellers to set up a shop and add product listings. If you aren't already a member, begin by registering for an account. Then click on "Sell on Etsy" to start.

The Etsy Seller Guide at etsy.com/seller-handbook will get you up and running using best practices from successful sellers.

YouTube offers hundreds of free tutorial videos on all aspects of setting up an Etsy store. Many of them will be trailers or lead magnets for paid courses. But you can get a lot of solid tips for free.

The best practices outlined in this chapter will help you set up your Etsy shop to succeed. Here you will learn about:

- Setup steps
- Product listings
- Images
- Etsy SEO
- Your product descriptions
- Share on social media
- Customer service
- Etsy ads
- If sales are poor
- Get reviews and publicity
- Etsy apps
- Mailing list

Setup Steps

* Brand your Etsy shop by naming it with your business name. The name shows up in your Etsy shop URL. Example: https://www.etsy.com/shop/YourBizName. You can shorten this URL for business cards using the free tool https://www.bit.ly/.

* Decide what you will sell and make a list of your products. Each product will have its own listing.

* Research popular keywords buyers use to find products like yours (EtsyRank.com).

* Write a description for each product.

* Take photos of your items from different angles. Etsy allows you to upload ten images for each product.

* Read and follow all the guidelines and store policies when setting up your shop.

Shop Info and Appearance

* Add your artist's story to your Seller's Bio. Shoppers want to know how you became an artisan.

* Your "Shop Announcement" gives you a place to add interesting details about your products and your creative process. It is also an area for placing popular keyword phrases used by Etsy shoppers.

* Design and upload a shop icon, profile image of yourself and (optional) store banner.

Shop Policies

* Write a welcome message. If natural, weave in popular search terms. They won't help you here with Etsy search rankings but will help you get found by Google.

* Create your Payment, Shipping, Refund, Seller, and Additional Information policies. Don't omit these as Etsy search favors shops with completed policies.

Improve Your Product Listings

* Product listings are pages that display information to viewers about your product. Listings include images, a title, a

product description, tags, price, shipping, quantity, and materials.

* When setting up a product listing, fill in each section. Each of the areas on the listing page provides another opportunity to appear in searches.

* Create more listings by copying your best-selling listings and changing the title for the copied listings. Use a different popular search term for each new listing. Be sure to change your tags to match your titles as much as possible. Copying listings complies with Etsy policies.

* More new product listings will help, too. Go back to Chapter 1 and think about how you might expand into new lines.

* If you have customer reviews, include them in your product listing description. Even though viewers can access your reviews elsewhere, repeating one or more of the best ones in the description adds social proof that your product is worth buying.

* Use all ten of the allowed images for each listing. Images play a major role when online shoppers browse your listings. Ninety percent of shoppers report that great photos played a part in their buying decision. Take photos of an item from different angles. Include images of people using your item and images of the product with a plain white background.

Etsy SEO

In the last chapter, you learned the basics of SEO. You saw keyword search terms used by buyers looking for specific crafts. Here we look at SEO tips to help your Etsy shop listings get found more often in searches.

Where to Place Keywords and Tags

Placing popular tags in your Etsy, Amazon, and other online shop product listing pages increases your chances of getting found in search. But be careful not to over use each tag. Once is plenty and a collection of related terms helps establish relevancy in the search engine algorithms.

Here are the areas where you can make use of tags in your product listings for SEO purposes:

- **Title**: The first 40 characters (first few words) of your title are the most important for SEO, so include the most popular buyer keywords at the beginning.
- **Description**: Your product description promises benefits to the buyer. Insert popular keywords and tags throughout.
- **Attributes**: Attributes are extra tags like colors and materials. People search for "red" scarves or "cotton" clothing.
- **"About" page**: Your artist's story is an often-overlooked area to include your keywords. Weave them into your personal narrative.
- **Shop announcement**: Yet another area where you can include popular search terms.
- **Tags**: Use all allowable tags. They should differ from each other. Optimally, tags should match as many of the words in your product's title as possible.
- **Categories**: Categories act like tags so choose categories relevant to your product line. But if you sell tables under the category "Furniture" don't waste one of your tags with the word "furniture."
- **Shop policies and terms**: Include your popular search terms in your policies content. This content gets read by Google and may appear in search results.

* Etsy allows you thirteen keyword tags for each listing. Use all of them. As much as possible, your listing's title should match your tags.

* Include related search terms in your product listing description.

* Shops with only a few items in a category rank lower in search compared to shops with many listings in the same category.

* Add new item listings to your Etsy store regularly, but not all at once. New listings get a slight boost in search rankings.

* Aim for a minimum of fifty to a hundred listings. Each listing is a new opportunity to be found in Etsy searches, especially if you use unique keywords and tags in each listing.

* Use Etsy's "Search analytics." Access it through Shop Manager > Marketing > Search analytics. It's not so useful for new sellers because there isn't much traffic or sales to analyze. But if you have been on Etsy awhile and made sales, the search analytics tool will tell you which search words shoppers used to find your items converted to sales. Search analytics revealed my shop was getting traffic for search terms I had not used in my tags or listing titles. I went back in and added the terms as tags in a few listings and sales increased.

Product Descriptions

* In your product descriptions, tell the customer how your item will transform their life. If applicable, how many ways can a person use your item?

* Spellcheck your listings before posting. When shoppers see misspelled words or grammatical errors, they may imagine your item is as carelessly assembled as your text.

* Add a shipping profile or select a shipping profile you want to update. Fill out the shipping profile. Select your order processing time (how long it will take to ship your order). The shorter the processing time, the more you will convert visitors to customers.

Share on Social Media

After you have posted your listings, it's time to share. Etsy makes it easy for you to share your product listings, five-star re-views, items that have been recently favorited, and special sales to your social profiles on Pinterest, Facebook, Instagram, and Twitter.

To make use of this feature, go to your Shop Manager > Marketing > Social Media and then look for the tab near the top that reads, "Social accounts." From there, connect your other social profiles. After you have connected your social profiles to Etsy, you are ready to post. Look for and click on the "+Create Post" button. Then Etsy walks you through creating and sharing a post to all your sites. Etsy's tool is free.

If posting frequently is taking too much of your time, schedule your social sharing with tools (subscriptions) like Buffer.com, Hootsuite.com or Tailwindapp.com.

How to Treat Customers

* When someone messages you through Etsy, respond quickly. It builds goodwill. When I get a message from an Etsy shopper with a question, I respond right away. Customers always thank me for my prompt reply.

* Etsy allows you to program a Thank You message that goes out automatically upon a sale. Express your gratitude for their purchase and tell them when they can expect to get their order.

* Another way to automate building customer relation-ships is to create a discount coupon for the next purchase. You have the option to set it to go to every customer upon checkout. Go to Shop Manager > Marketing > Sales and Coupons.

* If you get complaints, offer to replace the problem item or issue a refund. Put the customer in control. Don't make them feel they are wrong.

* Fix problems, even if doing so costs you extra. You've heard the saying, "the customer is always right." It has never been truer than with online sales.

* If you receive a negative review, get in touch with the customer and take care of any issues. After you have made things right, ask the disgruntled shopper to alter their negative rating. Offer a refund or substantial discount coupon if it means getting better feedback.

* Print and include a packing slip that Etsy creates for each order so customers know where the product is coming from. I write on it a big "Thank You" with the person's name at the top.

* Let shoppers know when they can expect their order to ship and make it as soon as you confidently can. Click Shop Manager > Settings > Shipping settings.

Etsy Ads

A way to potentially boost your Etsy sales is through their "Etsy Ads" feature under "Marketing" in your "Shop Manager," but only test "Etsy Ads" after you have had sales. This is because you want to know that your listing converts visitors to buyers before you put money into ads.

Choose listings you want to promote and set a daily spending budget. You can set your budget as low as $1 a day. Start with the minimum so you can affordably test results. After a few weeks, go back in and view your promoted listings statistics.

If you haven't read the chapter on pricing and calculated your profit margins, do it before testing any ads. You will need to know your margins before you can look at your stats to determine if you made or lost money through Etsy ads.

Etsy does the keyword analysis for the ads—you don't have to do anything except turn the "Etsy Ads" feature on, choose which listings you want to promote, and set a budget. You only pay when someone clicks through from an ad to your product listing.

If Sales Are Poor

* If your Etsy shop has been up for a while but is performing poorly, hire successful Etsy sellers to critique it. You can get shop reviews on Etsy for anywhere from $20 to $100 or more. Save money at Fiverr.com and search for "etsy review."

* When using Fiverr, only work with providers who have all five-star reviews. I bought three reviews because I wanted fresh perspectives of my shop. You might think all of them would offer the same suggestions. Though on some points they agreed, each of the reviewers gave unique ideas that helped my sales.

* Browse the community forums and teams (groups) on Etsy to learn and share experiences with other craft artists about setting up, marketing, and running an Etsy store.

* List more items. Increasing the number of your product listings can boost your sales. You'll have more pages through which shoppers can find you. And Etsy search appears to favor

shops that have more items than other sellers in the same category.

 * Run discount coupons for key shopping dates. Etsy provides you with a calendar of peak buying seasons with tips for tying in special offers. Go to Shop Manager > Marketing > Key shopping dates.

 * Boost sales by offering free shipping, if your profit margin allows it. Etsy created a seller option called Guaranteed Free Shipping for orders over $35. Sellers who opt in to the program get priority in search results over sellers who do not offer free shipping. You can also go into your Shop Manager > Marketing > Sales and coupons. By using Etsy's free shipping coupon (choose "no end date"), Etsy displays a free shipping badge on your shop's product pages. If you set up free shipping as a shipping option, you won't get the Etsy badge. The Etsy badge helps your listings show up better in search results. Even if you have to raise your prices to cover shipping, it will increase your visits and sales.

 * Funneling offline shoppers to your Etsy store helps you gather more reviews and build social proof. Over twenty percent of my Etsy buyers come from my business cards collected by shoppers visiting my craft show booths.

Get Reviews and Publicity

Shopping blogs and social media influencers seek new products to review. But the competition for getting reviews can be tough. Magazines, newspapers, and freelance writers also report on handmade products they think will interest their readers. See Chapter 11 for more about getting free publicity from influencers.

Etsy is great for learning how to set up and promote an e-commerce site for your handmade crafts. After you master Etsy selling, test other platforms or start your own website. The next chapter introduces more ways to sell online, including Handmade on Amazon.

CHAPTER 9

Alternatives to Etsy

Though Etsy may be the most popular market for hand-made products, there are other options to help you grow your sales and broaden your online presence.

Amazon Handmade is a category on Amazon available to their 300 million+ shoppers.

Sites like Artfire, Zibbet, and others also compete with Etsy to attract shoppers looking to buy handmade. Another option is setting up your own domain-name website.

Facebook offers Facebook Page owners the option to sell directly to users through Facebook Shops.

Pinterest gives sellers the ability to sell direct to browsers through a Shop link

With so many possibilities, you may feel you have to choose between them. But there is no rule that says you can only sell in one marketplace. Test each and measure the results. Then focus on all platforms that bring sales and healthy profit margins.

In this chapter, you will learn about:
- Selling on Amazon Handmade
- Alternatives to Etsy and Amazon
- Getting a domain-name website

Selling on Amazon Handmade

Amazon Handmade opened in 2015. Reviews by maker-sellers have been mixed. Those who have done well report better sales than Etsy, Other sellers say Etsy is better. If you test Amazon Handmade for your product line, give it two to three months and measure your results.

Applying and getting set up as a seller on Amazon Handmade is more complex than other online marketplaces for handmade products. The application link is: https://services.amazon.com/handmade/handmade.html.

If accepted, you must subscribe to their Professional Account for sellers. The monthly charge of around $40 was being waived for Handmade sellers as an incentive, but that could change by the time you read this book.

On the plus side, Amazon has a huge marketplace of buyers. Sellers get access to Seller Central, a back office with in-depth analytics and reports on how often your item was viewed, clicked on, and sold.

What to know about selling on Amazon Handmade:

* Seller fees are fifteen percent of the retail price. This is higher than Etsy's five percent. Calculate your profit margins before you sign up. (Check sites for current fee structure.)

* Setting up product page listings is straightforward. You can copy and paste most of the same elements used on your Etsy listings.

* Amazon Handmade gives you an Artisan's Profile, where you can paste in your artist's story and upload images of yourself.

* Amazon allows sellers to promote their handmade products through Sponsored Product ads. You can access reports that reveal which keyword searches result in sales. You can also learn how the cost of your ads compares to your sales. This lets you adjust your ads to run only those that result in a healthy profit margin.

* If your profit margin allows, consider FBA (Fulfilled By Amazon). For many wood crafts, this won't be practical. But for lightweight items, FBA can really boost sales. In FBA, you ship (at your expense) your products to Amazon warehouses. They fulfill orders to their more than ninety million Amazon Prime member buyers. Amazon Prime members get free shipping and buy more often than non-members.

* With 85% of Amazon shoppers reporting they hesitate to make a purchase because of shipping charges, offering free shipping sets you apart from most sellers.

* As with all e-commerce sites, SEO plays a big role in getting views and sales from a site's marketplace. Go to the Amazon Handmade category and start typing in words that describe your product. Amazon will start to auto-populate your search with suggested keywords. Those suggested words come from searches that have resulted in sales. The popular search terms on Amazon may differ from search terms used by Etsy shoppers.

* Place the most popular keywords at the beginning of your title and your product descriptions. Amazon allows for additional keywords—similar to Etsy tags—in each listing.

* You can also use a service like MerchantWords.com to discover buyer search terms. Starting from your own list of words and phrases, MerchantWords delivers a list of keywords you may not have thought of. You'll also see how strong the competition is for your products.

* Make customer service your top priority. Amazon shoppers weigh other buyer reviews before making purchases. Double-check your product and packaging quality before shipping. Be willing to refund an unhappy customer.

Alternatives to Etsy and Amazon

Though Etsy and Amazon Handmade have the largest buyer marketplaces for handmade products, there are other sites worth checking out. The top Etsy and Amazon Handmade alternatives in the US:

- Artfire.com
- BigCartel.com
- Zibbet.com
- IndieMade.com
- iCraftGifts.com
- eCrater.com
- Bonanza.com

Some seller sites charge a small percentage when a sale is made. Some charge a monthly or yearly fee and allow you to upload as many listings as you want. Each site has a different set of terms, so read the fine print to avoid surprises.

Setting Up Your Own Domain Site

Many sellers prefer having a domain-name website. With your own site, you are independent of whatever changes a large outfit like Etsy or Amazon makes.

One of the big complaints about Etsy, Amazon, and the other online shop providers is that they own the customers, not you. Setting up your own domain site lets you blog, capture e-mails, provide a customer newsletter, offer specials, announce new products, and otherwise operate like other e-commerce sites.

Building a site from scratch can be stressful and time-consuming. Using services and tools like Wix or WordPress allows you to set up a basic site in less than an hour.

Steps for DIY setting up a domain site:

* Your business name is the best choice for your domain name as it helps you brand your business. If you can't get the exact name, try adding a short word before or after your domain name and check for availability again.

* Once you settle on a name, register it at <u>NameCheap.com</u> or <u>GoDaddy.com</u>. The annual fee to keep your domain name is anywhere from $9 to $20, depending on the registrar.

* After you have registered your domain name, you need a web host. Some registrars also provide hosting. If not, there are thousands to choose from. HostGator.com and BlueHost.com have received good reviews.

* All web hosts walk you through connecting your domain name to their servers so that your website will be visible online.

* The next step is creating and uploading pages with content. Sellers usually include: home page, about the artist page, shopping page, contact page, subscribe page and a blog page if you plan to blog.

* WordPress, a free web-building application available from most web hosts, provides everything you need. It offers free themes, free e-commerce plugins and lots of free support. WordPress sites are popular for e-commerce and for blogging.

* If you aren't using WordPress with a shopping-cart plugin, you will need to build an online catalog and process transactions. Shopify and BigCommerce are two of the most popular shopping-cart programs.

Online Advertising

Ad campaigns or promoted listings have paid off for some sellers but not all. You can only know if they work for your products by testing. Limit your risk by setting a low daily budget for ad spending and an end date for a campaign.

Save yourself time and money. Don't test ads until you have sales. If you get sales organically, it means your product page is likely to convert shoppers who come through ads. But the reverse is also true. If your product page doesn't already produce sales, throwing money into ads is a waste.

As I have mentioned several times, know your profit margins if you intend to grow your business. Ads are one way to boost your sales, but there's no guarantee they will.

Before you start a campaign, determine how much you can afford and are willing to lose and then test ads. If your test ad campaign loses money, stop running the ads; if your test makes enough money that you still earn a profit from each sale, increase your ad spend / daily budget gradually, continuing to measure results.

Tips for Running Ads

- Ad options differ from site to site. Sometimes they are called "Promoted Listings."
- Test ad campaigns with a small daily budget.
- Run ads long enough to get 2,000 impressions.
- Measure click-throughs and cost of sales.
- If you have the budget, test different audiences.

- Drop ads that don't result in sales.
- Gradually increase ad campaigns that convert at low cost of sales, continuing to monitor spending vs. profit.

Just ahead, another way to market online is by publishing content on social media, which is mostly free except for the time you invest. promoting through social media takes finesse and time. Keep reading to discover best practices used by artisans to grow their social following.

Chapter 10

Promoting with Social Media

Social media offers multiple ways to grow a fan base for your handcrafted products. However, those active on each site are there for specific reasons and behave differently. For instance, Facebook fans respond to or engage with posts in one way, fans on Instagram another.

Handmade sellers spend time on social networking sites to gather followers, increase sales, and follow up with customers. Sellers can:

- Post product images and videos
- Learn what customers think and how they communicate
- Interact with customers to build relationships
- Grow their following
- Link more visitors to an Etsy shop or website
- Check out what competitors are doing to market their things
- Create, test and measure ads

To help you include social media marketing in your handmade business, this chapter covers:

- Social marketing tips
- Scheduling tools
- Moving followers over to your e-mail list
- Facebook tips
- Pinterest tips
- Instagram tips

Social Marketing Tips

Before we go into the four main social platforms, the following checklist acts as a primer for social posting:

* Get familiar with how a platform functions. People hang out on social sites for specific reasons. If you learn something that works to promote your Instagram posts, the same tactic may or may not work on Pinterest.

* Focus on learning a social site you like and feel most at ease with. Don't spread yourself thin by trying to be everywhere online.

* Don't expect big returns. Studies show that only 1% to 2% of social site referrals buy on their first visit to a site.

* Some sellers say Instagram sends them more customers. For others, it's Pinterest or Facebook. Which is best for you? Test some posts and measure your results.

* Brief posts with fewer than seventy characters get more interaction than longer posts.

* Post several times a day. Use tools described later in this chapter to schedule post deliverance across sites.

* In your posts, be helpful. Be inspiring. Be entertaining. Be educational.

* Posts with images get more shares on Facebook and the most retweets on Twitter.

* Posts with videos get the most engagement.

* Reply to people's comments on your posts. The more engagement you can get going, the more your posts will show up organically.

* How often should you promote your product when posting socially? Start out with seven posts that help, entertain or educate, and then post your product-related article or link. Repeat a few times and notice how your followers respond.

Scheduling Tools for Social Media Posts

Managing all of your profiles across several sites one at a time can quickly take up your day. In Chapter 8, Selling on Etsy, one of the tools in your Etsy Shop Manager under the Marketing category is the Social Media option. You can quickly connect and promote posts of your listings, reviews and favorites directly to your Facebook, Instagram, Pinterest, and Twitter profiles.

There are other scheduling tools (paid subscriptions) to help leverage your time. Try one or more for a month (some offer free trials) and then decide if you want to stay with that tool or try a different one.

- <u>Outfy.com</u>
- <u>Hootsuite.com</u>
- <u>Buffer.com</u>
- <u>Tailwindapp.com</u>
- <u>SproutSocial.com</u>

Build a Mailing List

If your favorite social site folds or changes policies, or if your account gets shut down, all of your followers and the work you did to get them vanishes. There is no back-up.

You may not own your social followers, but you own your mailing list. And that list will be yours to promote through regardless of what happens to your social platforms.

To get your followers to give you their e-mail addresses, offer an incentive like a coupon, free download, a newsletter subscription, or a mini course.

Your e-mail list is an asset. Back it up frequently. Use it to stay in touch with your tribe. See Chapter 13 for tips on capturing and making use of your mailing list.

Facebook Tips

Over two billion people use Facebook. Almost eighty percent of shoppers in the US have found products to buy while on Facebook. Once you have a personal profile set up on Facebook, you can set up a free Facebook page for your business. Facebook personal profiles are limited to adding 5,000 friends, but Facebook pages can have an unlimited number of likes and followers.

Selling from a Facebook Page

* FB pages let you add content about your products and sell them from the page. You also have access to "Insights" providing visitor data you can't get from a profile page. You will learn how many people your posts reached, how many new likes you got, how many people engaged with your posts, and more.

* Sell directly from your Facebook page by enabling a Facebook Shop tab in your page settings. In 2020, Facebook announced an upgrade to the Shop feature in line with being more competitive with Amazon and other e-commerce sites. Shoppers can browse your items, make a purchase, and pay for it while remaining on your Facebook page.

* Getting sales from Facebook means getting visual, big time. Studies show Facebook users respond more to imagery and video than simple text.

* Alternatively, the Shop tab can link to your other website or your Etsy shop. But sending customers away from Facebook creates an added step they have to take and will lower conversion rates.

* For a detailed video on setting up a Facebook Shop, see https://www.youtube.com/watch?v=EDqz32hr-1E

Posting Tips

* Post consistently; at least several times a week.

* Post from your FB Page, not your personal profile.

* Upload images of your products, videos of your creative process and posts with a mix of video, imagery, and text.

* FB users love video. Thirty percent of mobile FB users report that video is their favorite way to find new products.

* Facebook Live videos get six times as many interactions as regular videos. FB Live videos also rank higher in newsfeeds.

Facebook Stories

When you post to your FB page in the normal way, that post shows up in some but not all of your viewers' feeds. As a person's feed fills up with incoming posts, your message cycles down in the newsfeed as newer posts appear at the top.

FB stories appear above your users' feed and remain there for 24 hours. If you add to your story several times a day, it keeps your business name in front of your fans instead of it vanishing in the feed.

You can add stories to your FB page from your smartphone. They can include photos, videos, and text.

Stories work best as a "behind the scenes" look into your crafts business. For example, you might shoot a video of you making a new piece. Or, for fun, completely messing one up.

"Buy Sell" Groups on Facebook

* FB "Buy Sell" groups for handmade products allow you to post images, product descriptions, and links to your item's sales page on Etsy or elsewhere. Buyers join these groups to browse for handmade items. See Facebook.com/groups/craftsu.

* To find groups on FB to post your products in, type "buy sell handmade" or "buy sell crafts" in the search bar at the upper left of any FB page. Then click on the Groups tab to narrow results to only look at Groups.

* Facebook.com/marketplace/ is FB's own buy/sell market. It's used by 800 million people globally each month. Sellers list items for sale. Shoppers browse for bargains. Like with Craigslist, there is no fee to use the marketplace.

* FB Marketplace displays tons of stuff people are looking to get rid of at low prices. Search results are tailored to your local area.

* A search for "handmade" brought up hundreds of items near me. Most of the listings were pre-owned items. Some were new and priced at the same retail price the seller asks on Etsy.

* Though listing handmade products next to used stuff won't set your products apart, your item on FB Marketplace gives you a virtual shopping cart for free. You link directly to your product listing, buyers can pay through Facebook Payments, and you ship the item or deliver it locally.

Pinterest Tips

Pinterest.com is a visual search engine where you pin your favorite images and videos from across the web. Pins on Pinterest don't expire, so investing time here can pay off in the long term. The site gets over two billion searches each month. 93% of pinners use Pinterest for planning purchases.

For example, fans of Pinterest use it to search for how-to tips, what's in style in home decor, and much more. DIY is among the top interests on Pinterest. The average sale arising from a Pinterest search is close to $60—higher than average sales from Twitter or Facebook buyers.

Using EtsyRank's Trend Buzz report (mentioned in Chapter 1), here are a few trending searches on Pinterest. Do you make wood crafts that could fit into these popular search niches?

> bedroom décor: 167,252 searches
> living room décor: 146,497 searches
> home decor ideas: 141,074 searches
> teen room décor: 139,089 searches
> bathroom décor: 134,656 searches

* * * * * *

Pinterest Sends Visitors to Etsy

Not everyone who views your pins or follows you on Pinterest will click through to your online store, but enough do to justify investing time building a presence there. Pins don't disappear like Facebook posts. Even when neglecting to pin, my Etsy store statistics show visitors checking out my items from Pinterest almost every day. One of my pins from 2012 still sends traffic to my site.

* * * * * *

Setting Up Your Profile

* Choose the Pinterest business account option when registering. It offers more options including access to Pinterest Analytics, which tracks and measures how engaging your pins are.

* If you already have a personal profile, convert it to a business account for free.

* When setting up your profile, choose the same business name you use across all of your online sites.

* As with every place you sell online, include popular tags/ keywords related to your business in your profile description and when naming your boards so you get discovered in searches.

* Go to "Settings" and "Claim." Add your website if you have one. Also, claim your Etsy store, Instagram and YouTube accounts. Claiming your accounts gives you access to Analytics that show how visitors engage with your pins.

Creating Boards

* Pinterest boards let you organize your images by topics. After you have set up your profile, your next step is to create five to ten boards to place your pins in.

* Collect a mix of content browsers will enjoy looking through. For example, if you craft distressed looking signs in the home décor category, create one board for pins of your wood signs and another board with pins teaching people different ways to add a distressed look to their furniture.

* If you don't have a lot of product images of your own to fill in your boards in the beginning, fill them with images of related tips, guides, and products you like.

* Choose a popular keyword tag for the board name. Include a description using several related keywords. Upload an eye-catching cover image. Just as people judge a book by its cover, they explore your pins based on your boards' cover images.

* For examples of how to build out your boards, just search Pinterest using words that describe your products or customers; make a list of the most popular pinners and observe how they've created their boards and pins.

Gathering Followers

* Search for topics related to your products and find the most popular boards. When you find someone with a million or more followers, click the "Followers" link on their profile. A drop-down list appears. Start following the popular pinners' followers that appear to be active on Pinterest.

* Follow up to fifty new people every day. If you have set up your boards with interesting image collections, you will find popular pinners' followers following you. Pin new images daily as they show up in your new followers' feeds.

* Engage with your followers. Comment on their pins. Create conversations.

* Join Tailwind Tribes. Here you can join groups (tribes) of like-minded people. You share their posts and they share yours. See: https://www.tailwindapp.com/tribes.

Pinning

* Most Pinterest users are female and many of them are searching for home décor ideas.

* Pin consistently, even daily. Use a scheduling tool to make this easy.

* Pin images and videos. Pin helpful tips.

* Pinterest favors pins/pinners that get higher engagement with higher search results.

* Pinterest studies reveal that lifestyle images get more attention than product images, 150% more purchases than product photos alone.

* Videos pinned on Pinterest get higher engagement than other sites.

* Optimize pins to get more viewers from search. Each pin can have a description. In the description, use popular search terms and tags related to your products. Link directly to your product's listing on Etsy or elsewhere so viewers can click to buy instantly.

* As mentioned earlier, you can pin your Etsy listings, five-star reviews, and more on Pinterest through your Etsy Shop Manager.

* Rich pins are a special format that gives more context around an idea or product by displaying extra information on the pin. Rich pins are free, but your pins have to meet requirements and be approved. The steps for setting up rich pins are found at: help.pinterest.com/en/business/article/rich-pins.

* If you have a business account on Pinterest, you can access paid advertising through Promoted Pins. As with all ad campaigns, set your spending budget at the minimum dollar amounts, and test for two to three weeks. Pinterest provides ad tracking that reveals how many people view your ads and click through.

Instagram Tips

Instagram is a mobile-dominated platform for telling visual stories—98% of Instagram content comes from phones. While Instagram has over a billion users, 59% are under thirty years old. Many Etsy sellers report they get more sales via Instagram than Pinterest or Facebook. Understandable, since over 1,926,000 Instagram users follow Etsy's profile there.

Instagram members have a high engagement rate. Over 70% of users have bought something found there using their mobile phone.

Set Up an Instagram Account

* Download the Instagram app and install on your phone. If you plan to use Instagram to promote your handmade items, set up your new account as a business account or convert your existing profile to a business one.

* Like with other social sites, a business account allows you to promote or advertise your posts. You also get access to "Insights" (analytics) about your posts, hashtags, visitors, and engagements.

* Choose the same username (or a close variant if taken) that you use on Etsy and all your social media profiles. Upload the same profile image you use on other social sites.

* Include a link to your Etsy or other online shop in your profile.

Posting Images

* With the app open, take a photo with your phone, write a cute caption, and push "share." You have the option to add image-editing filters before you share your photos.

* The app automatically sizes your uploaded image to display on mobile devices. Horizontal (portrait) oriented images fit the screen well as most people naturally hold their phones horizontally.

* Sharing images comes with options. You can share to your other social media profiles. You can add hashtags. You can tag other people in the image. And you can add your location so viewers will know where the image was taken.

* You can also upload images from your computer.

* In your post you can add a brief caption. Caption text is found through search, so include relevant hashtags.

Videos

* Instagram lets you add and edit videos up to sixty seconds long. Videos can come directly from your phone or from content you have transferred to your phone from another source.

* Sellers can add a call to action at the end of a video. Just add a line of text in the last moments.

Instagram Stories

* Instagram stories, like FB stories, feature your photos and videos at the top of your follower's feeds. They remain there for twenty-four hours.

* Upload your story-behind-the-scenes of your handmade gig. Post stories about how you got started in your craft business, how you make your products, and what inspires you.

* Use the "poll" feature to ask your followers questions. Discover what they think about your stories.

Hashtags

* Hashtags are mashed-up phrases preceded by the # sign. Example: #handmade. The # sign turns the phrase into a

clickable link. Hashtags help your posts get found in search.

* Hashtags can help you uncover other sellers with products like yours.

* Multi-worded hashtags help you attract buyers instead of just researchers. If you make and sell home items, broad topic hashtags like #decor won't be as useful to you as more specific hashtags like #handmadefurniture, or #woodtray.

* Use apps to find hashtags related to your niche like keywordtool.io, displaypurposes.com, skedsocial.com, hashtagify.me, or all-hashtag.com. AutoHash is a mobile app that analyzes your images and suggests hashtags.

* You can add up to thirty hashtags when you post or comment, but adding so many looks spammy. The fix is to add a comment and include hashtags in the comment.

* Studies show posts with multiple hashtags get twice the amount of interaction with viewers.

* Mix your choice of hashtags among your posts and comments.

* Use one of your hashtags for your Instagram name.

* Look at the posts on the most popular profiles in your niche. See hashtags you had not thought of?

* After your profile has received likes, comments, and followers over time use the "Insights" feature in your business account to discover which hashtags brought the most traffic to your Etsy store or website.

* Find keywords by starting to type in the search bar at Instagram and note the auto-complete drop-down list of popular tags. Instagram's auto-complete comes from actual searches.

* Save all your hashtags in a text file or spreadsheet. Separate them by niches, products, people, or other categories. When you need hashtags, just go to your file and copy them.

* Use hashtags used by communities related to your product's niche.

Where to Place Hashtags

* As a sticker on your images and videos
* Your post's description

* Comments you leave
* Comments you get
* Your Instagram stories
* Your profile bio

Tips for Posting

* When someone likes or comments on your image posts, send them a thank you. It's a natural way to start a conversation.

* If your creative muse takes a vacation, post other people's content.

* Study the posts of the most popular Instagram profiles in your niche. Look for content that attracted the most comments. This is a way to get inspired for what you could post.

* Follow the followers of other sellers in your niche. If they appear to be frequent or recent posters, start liking their images. Many of them will follow you back.

* Follow Etsy sellers with complementary product lines to yours. Comment and like their content. Message them and see if they would like to cross-promote each other's lines.

* Post often. Uploading content twice a day has shown to increase followers. Use one of the social media scheduling tools described earlier.

* Instagram is highly social. Tagging others (adding @personsusername) can earn goodwill and increase your post comments.

Instagram Advertising

* Like with most social platforms, you can promote your Instagram posts through paid advertising. For business accounts, the "Insights" function provides clues about which of your posts make good candidates for promoting.

* Start off with a small budget and test. Target your ad to reach followers of popular sellers in your niche.

* As with all paid promotions, include a call to action. Make it clear what you want viewers to do: visit your Etsy shop, make a purchase, sign up for your newsletter, or other action.

* Monitor your Etsy shop stats closely when you run an

Instagram or other ad campaign. Your Etsy stats will tell you if you are getting traffic from Instagram or other social networks. If ads are working, increase your budget and try new audiences.

    * If your ads do not result in profitable sales, stop the campaigns. Change your content, or your offer, or your audience.

Chapter 11

Getting Mentioned by Influencers

Publicity, or public relations (PR), is attention given to a person or product by the media. With the right pitch, your handcrafted product could get mentions in popular blogs, Instagram feeds, Pinterest boards, podcasts, magazines, or other media that result in sales.

Is influencer marketing worth going after? Yes, publicity might increase visitors and sales at your website. Appearing in a magazine, popular blog, or on TV builds your brand credibility and social proof and can propel your sales to new heights.

Here you will learn how to get publicity based on your story. We'll cover:

- How to prepare before reaching out to the media
- Types of influencer media
- Where to find media contacts
- Tips for getting publicity

How to Prepare before Reaching out to Influencers

One study showed that ninety percent of journalists begin story research by searching online. If they find you and your story is newsworthy, they will write about you.

Before you reach out to a reporter, blogger, or product reviewer, prepare an online media kit. Here is a list of what your media kit should include:

* The first thing to get clear about is your message. What's your story, your background, your vision/mission? You need a

seven-word version, a one-paragraph version, and a longer complete bio of all you have accomplished that's relevant to your product line.

* A downloadable, bulleted fact sheet of who you are, what you do, where you live, when you got started, how you make your craft, and your contact information.

* "About me" page. The story of your background, education, awards, and anything pertinent to your craft. Avoid listing your complete job history unless a position specifically applied to developing your business.

* High resolution, professional-looking photos of you, you making your crafts, and several of your best-looking pieces.

* Video of you making or talking about your crafting process.

* News release about you and your work.

* Exhibit dates if you have art or craft shows lined up for the coming year.

* Previous media mentions: interviews, articles, press clips, or reviews.

* Awards or competitions you have won.

* List of ten or twelve sample questions for an interview.

* If you have them, include jokes or fun facts.

* Your contact information.

Types of PR

Publicity takes many forms including mention in newspapers, magazines, TV, and online media such as blogs, podcasts, videos, and social site posts.

If you make a good pitch and your photos are interesting, local newspapers, magazines, and TV affiliate stations are likely to mention you because you are part of the community. If you get written about in one or more media, mention it when pitching on other blogs and to social influencers.

Social Influencers

Influencers on Instagram, Facebook, Twitter, Pinterest and YouTube produce content for thousands—even hundreds of thousands—of followers. How do you find these opinion shapers?

Social monitoring tools like Heepsy.com and MightyScout.com locate them for you. Though they are subscription services, you can sign up for a month, find lists of influencers in your genre, download the lists and have plenty of contacts to pitch.

Newspapers and Magazines

Most major media like newspapers and magazines look for stories that inform, educate, provoke, or entertain their readers. When you can supply editors with news or stories that relate to the interests of their audiences, you have made their jobs easier. The key is pitching reporters that have covered stories like yours. Finding contact information for the media is described later in this chapter.

How to Pitch the Media

The job of editors, writers, reporters and producers is finding stories to develop for their audiences. They get lots of pitches from product sellers every day and reject most.

Media reporters can look at a pitch or news release and determine in seconds if it's right for their readers or viewers. The key phrase is "their readers or viewers." This is where most pitches fail. The message or product is too self-promotional or isn't a fit for their audience. If you want someone in the media to mention you, learn all you can about what stories they write about.

Start your pitch by letting the person know how you found them and why you enjoy their content. Follow with a paragraph or two and a link to a longer news release on your website's online media kit.

Your pitch should be a brief enough introduction to your story that the editor is intrigued but not overwhelmed with too much information. State a problem that your handcrafted piece solves, like its function in the home or office. Include a link to your website, Facebook page, or blog for more information.

Part of your story is visual, so you will want to include your best images and/or video if you have it. If the person you are pitching wants to know more, they will contact you.

Where to Find Media Contacts

Media contacts could be writers, reporters, bloggers, producers, podcasters, and editors. There are many ways to find them.

As mentioned earlier, Heepsy and MightyScout are two of the many social listening tools offering both free and paid subscription options. Use them to find influencers by their audience, reach, and engagement.

Twitter.com helps you locate editors, producers, bloggers, and reviewers. In the search bar, type in the name of the media and hit enter. Then choose the "People" tab. For example, typing HGTV brings up show producers and reporters and what topics they cover. Also search by job title. For instance, search for "product reviewer" and start following reviewers who cover products like yours. A survey reported that forty-six percent of journalists receive story pitches through Twitter.

Print magazine mastheads are typically found in the first pages. It's the section that lists the publisher, editor and other staff including editors who cover specific sections like New Products, Startups, etc.

USNPL.com is a free-to-access directory of newspaper reporters in the US.

HelpAReporter.com (HARO) is a free newsletter sending out lists of media reporters looking for stories on a vast variety of topics. You can subscribe to receive one or more lists around broad topics.

More Tips for Getting Publicity

* Follow and read the news feeds, blogs, or watch the TV shows to which you are thinking of pitching your story.

* Target media outlets and reporters relevant to your work. If you make wood letters for kids, don't contact a writer for *Rolling Stone*.

* Discover if they have already reviewed businesses like yours.

* Search for the "New Products" section of a publication. These departments are always looking for cool new stuff for their readers.

* Pictures and videos tell stories. Reporters look for interesting visuals accompanying news releases.

* Whenever you come out with a new product, send out a news release. Send a product sample to local newspapers and TV networks.

* Announce any awards you have just won. Local newspapers like to feature independent businesses that receive recognition as it looks great for the community.

* Write a story if where you work is in a historic or unusual location.

* Take advantage of holiday gift buying. Feature editors look for stories ahead of holidays.

* Can you relate your items to special days or months? November 15 is America Recycles Day. Find more interesting facts about each month of the year at gone-ta-pott.com/facts-about-each-month-directory.html.

* Donate a piece you make to a charitable cause or charity fundraiser. Send a news release to local newspapers, magazines, and TV shows with a photo of your piece.

* Sponsor a local community event and publicize it to local newspapers.

* Reporters are always looking for news items that tie into what's being read and talked about in the mainstream media. Can you link a popular topic to your product line?

* At the end of your pitch to the media, link to your online media kit.

Start collecting any mentions of you by influencers or the media. For one thing, it will make you really proud of what you are creating. This collection should appear in your website's media kit. If you plan to grow your brand and sell to galleries and stores, you'll find a portfolio of press clippings can be very persuasive when approaching buyers.

When you want to scale a side hustle into a larger business, selling wholesale is the way to go. But it isn't for everyone. Keep reading to discover if building a wholesale operation is right for you.

CHAPTER 12

How to Sell Wholesale

Wholesaling means selling to stores, galleries, and catalogs who then mark up the price and sell your products to their customers.

Wholesaling allows you to grow your business by getting stores and others to sell your pieces while you stay home and focus on making them. The tips here will help you build relationships with one or as many store owners as you can handle.

Though the potential for scaling your business upward through selling wholesale is huge, there is a price that comes with expansion. It means you will spend increasingly more of your time managing others and less time making products. This includes training others. It means double-checking each item before shipping to make sure every piece was made with attention to details. It means calculating profit margins to the penny.

In this chapter, we will look at what it means to get involved in selling to stores like:

- Preparing to sell wholesale
- Finding wholesale buyers
- Working with stores, galleries, and interior designers
- Overlooked retail outlets

Preparing to Sell Wholesale

Know Your Profit Margin

In Chapter 4 on pricing, you learned how to determine your profit margin and whether you can sell your items wholesale.

Normally, if your production cost is one-fourth (or lower) of the store's retail price, you will make a profit wholesaling. If a store's retail price for an item is $200, your total production cost should be $50 or lower.

Production Capacity

How many items can you produce in one week? Is your production consistent and predictable? Stores like to show off new work. Can you come up with fresh product ideas every year or even more often?

Establish Your Terms

When a store buyer asks your terms for wholesale accounts, you need a handout with something like:

* * * * * *

Example: Wholesale Terms

Net 30 terms available with approval upon your third order. Opening orders are prepaid via Visa, Mastercard, AmEx, Discover or PayPal or company check (with seven business day delay). Orders ship insured within three days via UPS or Priority Mail from Santa Fe, NM to addresses throughout US. Opening minimum order: $300, minimum reorder: $150. Prepaid orders of $250+ get free shipping to US addresses. Products are sold on a non-returnable basis. While rare, any defective merchandise may be returned at my expense within 14 days of delivery.

* * * * * *

What Store Buyers Like

Be professional. Your business can be new but should show signs you are serious about it. At the minimum, store buyers expect you to have a brand or business name, wholesale terms, catalog sheets of your work, and an artist's story.

It's helpful to have a portfolio you can show them of your work, other shops or galleries carrying your work (not in their immediate area), and any media coverage you may have gotten.

Finding Wholesale Buyers

Visit stores: Ever walked by a shop you would like to see your pieces in? Go in and talk to the owner, unless the person is with a customer. In which case, quietly wait until they are free. Ask if you can make an appointment to show them your portfolio. If they aren't busy, they may want to look right then.

LinkedIn.com: Locate buyers online through LinkedIn. When searching the term "gallery buyer," LinkedIn showed thousands of profiles.

Selling to interior designers? Apply to join the American Society of Interior Designers LinkedIn group at https://www. linkedin.com/company/american-society-of-interior-designers/

Other LinkedIn groups for furniture makers: http://righton-nobull.com/blog/2012/05/the-top-linkedin-groups-for-furniture-industry-professionals/ .

Wholesale buying portals. The websites below act as online portals where independent retail store buyers can purchase directly from makers. Each site has its own terms for listing products:

- ArtfulHome.com (Trade Professional program)
- Stockabl.com
- Tundra.com
- Faire.com
- Indieme.com
- Wholesaleinabox.com

At craft shows, store buyers find you: I have displayed my handmade items at highly competitive craft shows, some attended by hundreds of thousands of shoppers. At the better shows, I typically pick up one new store account just from buyers or owners shopping at such events for new products.

Working with Stores, Galleries and Interior Designers

When working with stores face-to-face, increase your success rate by:

- Be on time for appointments. Don't show irritation if they are running late and need you to wait a bit.
- Have a portfolio of your best pieces, price lists, and business cards with you.
- Show interest in the owner's store. They will appreciate compliments.
- Ask questions. Buyers are usually happy to share advice with product makers. Ask them what wood crafts their customers are buying.
- Not every buyer you approach will buy. If you get a "no" be graceful and ask if the buyer has any suggestions about how to improve your work.
- Stay in touch with your buyers. They carry many items from many makers. They could run out of one of your products and only remember to order when you check in to learn how they are doing.
- It is acceptable in wholesale to ask for payment at the time of a store buyer's first order; some makers ask for payment for the first two orders. After the initial purchase(s), be prepared to extend credit to your store account for thirty days. This is commonly called net 30.
- If a buyer isn't pre-paying, ask for a purchase order number at the time they place an order. A purchase order is your proof that they placed an order.
- What do you do after you have extended credit and the account does not pay? Remain calm. Avoid calling the store and angrily demanding payment. Remind

them politely that you cannot ship more products until they pay the outstanding invoices. If they haven't paid in ninety days, send a more strongly worded letter that asks for them to take care of the past due bills before you turn to a collection agency.

- Most shipping services like UPS, FedEx Ground, and the U.S. Postal Service provide tracking numbers when you ship through them. This is your record that the buyers received the packages, in case there's any dispute.

- Stores usually pay shipping charges. Add this amount on to the invoice when billing.

- Encourage buyers to pay up front; offer free shipping when they pay at the time they order. This is a big saving for them and many will jump on it. Know your profit margins and determine if you can afford to offer this perk.

- If you plan on doing craft shows in the same cities where you have store accounts, make your retail prices the same as the stores'.

- Set up a secure shopping cart to process wholesale orders online. This makes it easy for your store buyers to order and speeds getting payments to you.

- Businesses, organizations, and individuals hire interior designers to arrange their living or business spaces and find items to place there. Get your products in front of home and office interior buyers at houzz.com and art-fulhome.com.

Overlooked Ways to Sell Wood Crafts

Selling online and to retail stores aren't the only outlets for wood crafts. Depending on what you make, check out these alternative markets:

- Gift shops at airports, hotels, museums, hospitals, and marinas carry handmade items. Locate gift shops in the US at gift-shops.regionaldirectory.us and in the UK: directory.independent.co.uk/gift-shops/in/uk.

- Campgrounds at national parks and tourist areas usually have gift shops. See reserveamerica.com/campgroundDirectory.do.
- Mail-order catalogs can also be a market for your handmade products. One of the most popular for handmade items is the Sundance Catalog, started by Robert Redford. Neiman Marcus publishes a holiday catalog that showcases fine handcrafted items. The Vermont Country Store and Coldwater Creek catalog offers handmade interior accessories and gift ideas.
- Forge relationships with building contractors, real estate agents, and architects. Any professional involved in home building can be a source of referrals for your home décor and furniture projects. A woodworking friend got high-paying projects from an art broker, who was well connected to million dollar home interior designers.

All the marketing tactics we've covered in this book can help get your products in front of more buyers. But even if someone doesn't buy from you the first time they find you, capturing their e-mail address gives you the ability to send a newsletter or follow-up messages with special offers and updates about your business. The next chapter teaches you how to grow and follow up with a mailing list of followers.

Chapter 13

Growing Your Customer List

A mailing list makes it easy to market to people or stores who have bought from you before. As mentioned in the chapter on social media, no matter how large your online following, you don't own them. Your follower list belongs to Facebook, Instagram, Pinterest, or other site. If something happens to your account or to the site, you lose them.

With an e-mail list, you can contact your customers regularly. A mailing list is a valuable asset. A study by the US Consumer Affairs Department says for every marketing dollar you spend to keep a current customer, you'll spend five dollars to get a new one.

Building a craft business with staying power isn't just about making sales, it's about creating lasting relationships. Today, when I was writing this, I got my fourth order from a returning customer on Etsy. She typically buys five or six pieces for herself and as gifts. Over time, I always include a free item when shipping her order, along with a thank you message. It has built good will and earned positive reviews on Etsy.

This chapter explores the many ways to stay connected with your customers and coax them into lifetime loyalty. Learn the importance of:
- Capturing and working with e-mails
- Excuses to follow up
- How to treat customers well

Growing an E-mail List

When you make a sale at a crafts fair or online, ask your customer if she would like to be on your mailing list. Many will say yes because they just found something from a seller they like. Take advantage of their enthusiasm. Even when a shopper shows interest but doesn't buy, the next best thing is to get them on your mailing list.

As mentioned earlier, when promoting on social media sites like Instagram, Facebook, Pinterest, or elsewhere, capturing e-mail addresses should be one of your goals.

Tools for capturing and managing customer e-mails

The following tools help you capture e-mails and manage your mailing list. You can create a series of autoresponders or send out a special offer or let your customers know about a new product you are launching: Aweber.com, Mailchimp.com, Getresponse.com, and Convertkit.com.

These tools also allow you to personalize e-mails to get a better response. An example is an e-mail addressed to a person by first name in the e-mail subject area and with the person's name included in the body text of the e-mail. One study showed that personalized e-mails generated over 400 percent more sales on average than non-personalized e-mails.

Five tips for e-mail:

1. Improve your response rates by letting people know in the e-mail subject area and in the opening text of the e-mail the reason you are writing to them.
2. People are busy, so get to the point of your message right away, whether it's letting them know about a special saving, a new product offer, or a craft show you will be exhibiting at in their area.
3. Remind customers of who you are and your previous relationship with them.
4. Send e-mail only to those people who have given you permission.
5. When someone asks to be removed from your list, do it. Avoid getting pegged as a spammer. You can lose your account and face criminal charges if found to be in violation of the CanSpam Act.

Excuses to Follow Up

The average cost of getting new customers is six to ten times the cost of staying in touch with current ones. When you can't think of a reason to reconnect with your contacts, here are excuses to reach out and remind people of you.

- Thank someone for visiting your booth at an event
- Thank your customer after each sale
- Announce a special sale
- Announce a contest
- Announce a new product release
- Send a product sample
- Advise about discontinued items
- Send a gift
- Learn if a customer got their order
- Learn if a customer got your letter, flyer, or communication
- Send a newsletter
- Send a postcard or flyer with a schedule of your upcoming shows and exhibits
- Send a product tip sheet
- Send a product catalog
- Ask for a referral
- Thank someone for a referral
- Offer a coupon or incentive to get customers to come back
- Offer to link to someone's website from your own
- Make your customer feel important by creating a preferred customer offering
- Send a news clipping or copy of an article appearing about you
- Share ideas for holiday gifts and special occasions
- Send interesting facts about the piece a customer bought
- Seek a host for a home party or trunk show
- Thank someone for sponsoring a home party or trunk show

- Send a customer survey asking for feedback on how you measured up for service and quality of product
- Encourage more orders by sending testimonials from satisfied customers
- Send cards celebrating holidays other than Christmas—like Mother's Day, Graduation, Thanksgiving and Valentine's Day

Create a follow-up calendar scheduling the above action steps so you have a plan for staying in touch.

Treat Customers Well

Customers talk to their friends about their shopping experiences, especially when they feel they've been treated badly. On average, an unhappy customer tells seven to fifteen others about their negative experience.

Customers are more likely to leave a negative review when they have a bad experience than take time to write a positive review. Since reviews are the fuel for online sales, make it a priority to fix customer issues immediately to avoid getting bad reviews.

Customers are five times more likely to stop doing business with someone because of mistreatment than because of any other reason.

Building and maintaining your customer list is one of many important practices covered in this book. It's one of many ways to market your handmade wood crafts. As you find your business growing, remember to monitor the bottom line. The next chapter gives you several ways to boost your profit margins.

CHAPTER 14

Improving Your Profit Margins

A s explained in Chapter 4 on pricing, profit margin is the difference between your costs and your revenues. Without healthy margins, your venture can't thrive or grow. Successful businesses, even those that are profitable, remain on the lookout for ways to improve.

There are two places in your business to look at where you can improve profits. You can (1) lower costs and/or (2) raise prices. This chapter gives tips for doing both.

Increase Productivity

Organized planning is the first place to look for decreasing time spent per project and increasing quality of production. There is no shortage of free and paid wood project plans online, including Youtube videos. Every minute you can save and still produce quality finished products, the higher your profit margins.

The following are a few woodworking resources for speeding up production:

- http://www.hardwooddistributors.org/postings/8-woodworking-tips-to-boost-your-efficiency
- https://www.woodworkingnetwork.com/wood-100/wood-100-winners/22-tips-enhance-production-wood-100-strategies-success
- https://www.woodmagazine.com/ideas/wood-shop-showcase/erik-jorgensen-woodworking-workstations
- https://www.pinterest.com/akesseler86/woodworking-shop-tips-tricks-techniques-and-mainten/

As your craft business grows and you bring in help, teach your employees or independent contractors how you want your items made using faster and smarter techniques.

Buy Used Tools

Woodworkers have a lot of investment in tools. Though there's a good case to be made for buying new equipment, if you are starting out on a tight budget, here are ways to cut costs:

- Scan listings on Craigslist.org. You can save a ton of money buying second hand tools and equipment on Craigslist.
- Buy tools at garage sales and flea markets: Find used equipment at flea markets and garage sales. But be careful with vendors at flea markets as they often buy bulk supplies made in China which don't last.
- Sales at Woodworkers Supply, Harbor Freight, Hobby Lobby, Michaels and Joann's: Get the mobile apps for these major retailers as they regularly send out discount codes.

Raise Your Prices

Makers just starting to sell their work typically under price their products thinking they will attract more buyers. But in the handmade marketplace, lowering prices more often lowers the perceived value and causes shoppers to turn away.

Price is not the top buying criteria in the handmade marketplace, except where there are many competitors for low-dollar items like T-shirts. What is true more often is that the quality of your work, how-when-where you display it, your packaging, and your artist's story can positively increase your sales.

Below are things you can do to raise the perceived value, which will allow you to increase your prices and boost your sales.

- **Look for better paying markets**. Where you sell affects how you price. You can ask and get more money for a fine woodworking piece selling to an interior designer than at a local farmer's market.

- **Raise prices until sales drop**. Shoppers of handmade items look at an item's price tag and decide about the item's value. If the price is too low, a shopper thinks the item is inferior. Many makers, including myself, have found that raising an item's price boosts sales. The way to test this is to take an item that is selling and raise the price a little. Keep raising prices every few weeks until sales drop off. Then go back to the last price where sales were steady.

- **Tell shoppers it's handmade**. State it in your marketing messages. When selling at events in your state, add "Handmade in _____ (your state)."

- **Display your wood crafts as if they were art**. When doing events that allow for electricity, use spotlights aimed on your top-selling pieces. Hang items along a backdrop wall or pro-panel wall, as if they were in a gallery. I found that when I set up my craft show display to look my store walls, shoppers appreciated my work more and did not hesitate to buy as I was testing for an optimum price.

- **Display your artisan story**. Stories add a human element while enhancing perceived value. Write about how you got into your craft and where you work. Explain what went on behind the scenes to produce an item. Describe your personal journey or evolution with your skill as a maker.

- **Improve your finishing touches**. Adding finishing touches to your wood crafts improves their perceived value.

- **Make Earth-friendly products**. If you use environmentally friendly materials, use words in your product signage and descriptions to remind shoppers that your products are eco-friendly or sustainable (only when any of these are true); multiple surveys report shoppers will pay more for environmentally friendly products (Fortune).

- **Use eye-catching, eco-friendly packaging**. Use biodegradable or recycled packaging like branded boxes, ribbons, or wrapping. Shoppers often buy a product's package as much as the contents and they have become increasingly conscious of the environmental impact of their purchases.
- **Personalize the product**. Customers expect to pay more to have a personalized gift they can give to someone special. The number of shopper searches for personalized handmade gifts grew over 22% on Etsy in 2019. Raise prices for customization.
- **Offer free shipping**. This tip is for woodcrafters of lightweight items. Survey after survey reports that the number one thing shoppers want when shopping online is free shipping. Eighty-eight percent of Amazon shoppers reported that free shipping draws them to shop there.

I look at my prices, sales, and expenses several times a year with the above in mind. If I can lower my costs or raise my prices, it brings in a little extra money to do more marketing. Improving your profit margins is one of the ongoing tactics for crafting a successful woodworking business. The next and final chapter outlines more key takeaways from this guide.

CHAPTER 15

Key Takeaways

Having sold my work through art-craft fairs and public events, Etsy, Handmade on Amazon, stores and galleries, private commissions, and my own gallery/giftshop, I observed a pattern of what works and what doesn't. This chapter sums up the most important areas of your business to pay attention to:

1. Choose products to make that are in demand. You may have good luck selling your own unique products. If so, keep going with it. However, if you are stuck for product ideas, review Chapter 1. Make your own creative version of products for which there is a proven demand.

2. Trust your creativity, but test the marketplace before investing heavily in a new idea. No matter how great you and your mom think your products are, the test is whether shoppers will buy them. Test before you invest.

3. Don't let competition intimidate you. There wouldn't be other sellers unless there was a demand. If I had let concerns about competition stop me, my handmade products would never have seen the light of day. As an artisan, you can craft your own style or product lines that wins a loyal customer base.

4. Know your production costs. Do the math. Numbers don't lie. You have to make a profit to sustain any venture, especially if you plan to scale up by selling wholesale. Review Chapter 4 for tips on pricing.

5. If your profit margin is too low, increase your item's perceived value so you can raise your prices. Price your items according to how much shoppers will pay.

6. Photograph your products as if they would appear on the cover of a magazine. It may cost you to get fabulous photos, but if you are selling online or creating a portfolio to approach wholesale buyers with, it is your images that make the sale.

7. Position fine crafts in front of buyers with money. You aren't competing with WalMart and you aren't selling to folks looking for a bargain. The high dollar markets for wood crafts include galleries and interior designers. On Etsy and Amazon Handmade, "buy handmade" isn't just a phrase, it's a consumer movement.

8. Display and package your items as if you are already a successful brand. Put attention on crafting a brand. Work on your artisan story, create a logo, clean up your marketing materials so everything looks consistent--from your business card to your website. Come across as professional and you can ask and get higher prices.

9. Scale up by selling wholesale or growing online. There are only so many craft shows a person can do. If you want to grow, you can gradually get more and more store accounts or increase your online sales and hire help for increasing production. See Chapter 12.

10. Listen to your customers. Their comments will tell you what to make and how you should make and display your products. You may resist what they tell you, but if you hear the same comment more than once, pay attention.

11. Follow your passion. I absolutely love making stuff by hand and my customers tell me they love my work. When you love what you do, fresh opportunities open up to you. You persist in the face of obstacles. You have a business and a life.

Consistently work to improve the eleven core elements above and your products will attract a tribe of loyal customers.

A successful business is like a finely crafted project, it takes time, attention to details, and lots of love. A year or two from now, it may not look anything like your vision of it today.

Wishing you the best in your wood crafting venture!

About the Author

James Dillehay is a craft artisan, former gallery owner, and author of twelve books. He has sold his handmade products at competitive juried shows in the US, in galleries and stores from Manhattan to the Grand Canyon, and online at Etsy, Ebay, and Amazon.

James has been interviewed in *The Wall Street Journal Online, Yahoo Finance, Bottom Line Personal, Family Circle, The Crafts Report, Working Mothers, Entrepreneur Radio, HGTV's The Carol Duvall Show*, and more.

He has developed and presented crafts marketing programs for the University of Alaska, Northern New Mexico Community College, Bootcamp for Artists and Craftspeople, and The Learning Annex.

He currently lives, writes, and creates cool stuff from a studio he built himself (and it doesn't leak) next to a national forest in New Mexico.

What's Your Next Step?

The question I get asked most is "how much should I charge for my craftwork?" Without a smart pricing strategy, it's almost impossible to succeed in the handmade marketplace.

Problem solved with the book: ***How to Price Crafts and Things You Make to Sell***—formulas and successful craft business ideas for pricing on Etsy and selling to stores, at craft shows and everywhere else.

It may well be the most useful guide you own for your maker business.

<u>Buy on Amazon now!</u>